The Mechanics of True Worship

The Mechanics of True Worship

by Charles Dixon

BOGOTA, NEW JERSEY

The Mechanics of True Worship

Copyright © 1996 by Charles Dixon. First Printing. Printed and bound in the United States of America. All rights reserved. No portion of this book may be reproduced in any form or by any means, including information storage and retrieval systems, without written permission from the publisher, except by a reviewer, who may quote brief passages in a review. Published by END TIME WAVE PUBLICATIONS, P.O. Box 141, Bogota, New Jersey 07603-0141.

ISBN 0-9634306-7-X

Unless otherwise indicated, all Scripture quotations are from the King James Version of the Bible. Scripture quotations marked (NIV) are taken from the *HOLY BIBLE, NEW INTERNATIONAL VERSION*, Copyright © 1973, 1978, 1984 by International Bible Society. Used by permission of Zondervan Publishing House. All rights reserved.

The "NIV" and "New International Version" trademarks are registered in the United States Patent and Trademark Office by International Bible Society. Scripture quotations marked (AMP) are taken from *The Amplified Bible, Old Testament*, Copyright © 1965, 1987 by the Zondervan Publishing House. *The Amplified New Testament*, Copyright © 1954, 1958, 1987 by The Lockman Foundation. Used by permission.

Those marked (NASB) are from the *New American Standard Bible*, Copyright © 1960, 1962, 1963, 1968, 1971, 1972, 1973, 1975, 1977 by The Lockman Foundation, La Habra, California. Used by permission.

Verses marked (TLB) are taken from *The Living Bible*, Copyright © 1971. Used by permission of Tyndale House Publishers, Inc., Wheaton, Ill. 60189.

Note: In some Scripture quotations, italics have been added by the author for emphasis only.

Typesetter: Sheila Chang

Contents

Dedication		vii
Introduction		ix
I	The Progressive Climb to Worship	1
II	Prerequisites of Worship	11
III	Sacrifices, Offerings & Rituals	31
IV	Let Us Worship Him	53
V	The Difference Between Praise and Worship	61
VI	To Whom Should We Direct Our Praise?	107
VII	Who Can Praise The Lord?	117
VIII	Scriptures That Reveal Who Can Praise The Lord?	127
IX	More Scripture References	131
X	A Prayer For You	155

Dedication

I wholeheartedly dedicate this book to you, my lovely wife, Lydia and my awesome children, Priscilla and David. I thank God for giving you guys to me. You guys are the best. I thank you for being so supportive of me and displaying the spirit of patience as I do the work that God has given me to do. I pray and believe in my heart that God is well pleased with you and will reward you all for your great labor of love. Through God, you have allowed me to be a great husband and a great father. I love you greatly! Thank you again and know that I will always continue to love you.

Also, I dedicate this book to all the *true worshippers* of the Body of Christ. I believe that this is an hour where true worship is being restored in every aspect and a renewed excitement has hit the beach of the Church! For all who have embraced this excitement, who hunger to pursue God's presence and worship Him, I dedicate this book to you.

INTRODUCTION

Reverential devotion and allegiance pledged to God are the hallmark of successful Christian living. The rituals or ceremonies by which this reverence is expressed is in the form of worship. The word worship is derived from the Old English word "worthship," which denotes the worthiness of the one receiving the special honor or devotion. Worship is the attitude and acts of reverence to a deity. The term worship itself in the Old Testament comes from the Hebrew word which means to bow down, or prostrate oneself, a posture indicating reverence and homage given to a lord, whether human or divine.

Today, there is an urgent call echoing out the very trumpets of God. Sure, we must continue to heighten and increase our levels of studying God's Word and, sure, we must enlarge our own prayer and fasting lives, but there's a clarion call which says we must worship He Who has created us!

I have come to find out that there are many more of us in the Body of Christ who desire to be a doer of the Word and not just a hearer only. But our greatest stumblingblock is in our attempts to accomplish the "How Tos." We have found that we have spent years and countless hours of studying, learning and identifying the what, where and when and why of the things of God. I believe that we the Church have done well to accomplish these areas. It is now our season to amass the "How tos" of everything we've learned. "Yes, I believe I need to pray. But how do I pray? I want to act in faith. But how do I exercise my faith? I realize I must worship the living God. Please show me how."

The exclusiveness of a watch made by the Hamilton Corp. is not due to the external parts that we see, but the far greater internal workings of the watch. It is the internal of a thing where its beauty and strength lie. These inner workings are the mechanics. This book is not an attempt to simplify this awesome task and tool that our Heavenly Father has given us— to worship. This book is to bring a greater level of clarity to the very mechanics of what we know to be true worship. I have taken the time to examine these mechanics, since God is looking for true worshippers; we must know true worship.

The Body of Christ is now living in an hour where it has discovered the ineffectiveness and inadequacy of mere knowledge of God through His Word, or even of their covenantial relationship and dedication to Him. We are faced with a realization that no matter how much we operate in just these arenas, we must be honest with ourselves and admit that our hearts can remain yet cold toward our Father. The act of love toward Him may still be obsolete.

A solidified relationship with the Lord does include the knowledge of Him, a dedication to him, but also a worship of Him. These three ingredients represent the love of God in its totality. If the relationship is to reach a mature level, all three ingredients must be present in equal measure. The three work in a synergistic way. True worship will bring on a deeper knowledge of Him and a dedication to Him and vice-versa.

Charles Dixon, Ph.D
May 1996

CHAPTER I

THE PROGRESSIVE CLIMB TO WORSHIP

ABRAHAMIC WORSHIP

Now the Lord had said unto Abram, Get thee out of thy country, and from thy kindred, and from thy father's house, unto a land that I will shew thee:

And I will make of thee a great nation, and I will bless thee, and make thy name great; and thou shalt be a blessing:

And I will bless them that bless thee, and curse him that curseth thee: and in thee shall all families of the earth be blessed.

So Abram departed, as the Lord had spoken unto him; and Lot went with him: and Abram was seventy and five years old when he departed out of Haran.

And Abram took Sarai his wife, and Lot his brother's son, and all their substance that they had gathered, and the souls that they had gotten in Haran; and they went forth to go into the land of Canaan; and into the land of Canaan they came.

And Abram passed through the land unto the place of Sichem, unto the plain of Moreh. And the Canaanite was then in the land.

And the Lord appeared unto Abram, and said, Unto thy seed will I give this land: and there builded he an altar unto the Lord who appeared unto him.

And he removed from thence unto a mountain on the east of Beth-el and pitched his tent, having Beth-el on the west, and Hai on the east: and there he builded an altar unto the Lord, and called upon the name of the Lord.
Genesis 12:1-8

We can trace very early elements of worship in the Bible. There are occasions where individuals like Abraham were found building an altar and calling on the name of God— worshipping. In Genesis, chapter 12, we see that God told Abraham to "get thee out of." In other words, Abraham received a call to separate himself. God will always call us to separate from something to something. In verses 2 and 3, God begins to paint a picture of promises being granted if Abraham would be obedient and separate. Verse 4 shows us that he was indeed obedient. The act of worship is always tied into an act of obedience. Here we see Abraham receiving a command and obeying it. Then he next begins to worship God. As a result of his obedience and worship, God blesses Abraham with tremendous promises.

> **And the Lord said unto Abram, after that Lot was separated from him, Lift up now thine eyes, and look from the place where thou art northward, and southward, and eastward, and westward:**
>
> **For all the land which thou seest, to thee will I give it, and to thy seed for ever.**
>
> **And I will make thy seed as the dust of the earth: so that if a man can number the dust of the earth, then shall thy seed also be numbered.**
>
> **Arise, walk through the land in the length of it and in the breadth of it; for I will give it unto thee.**
>
> **Then Abram removed his tent, and came and dwelt in the plain of Mamre, which is in Hebron, and built there an altar unto the Lord.**
>
> **Genesis 13:14-18**

Following hearing his tremendous promise, Abraham remembers where his strength lies. Verse 18 tells us that he once again built an altar—worshipped God. Fortunately for Abraham and others of that day, this worship of God did not require an elaborate priesthood or ritualistic effect.

MOSAIC WORSHIP

> **And he said unto Moses, Come up unto the Lord, thou, and Aaron, Nadab, and Abihu, and seventy of the elders of Israel; and worship ye afar off.**
>
> **And Moses alone shall come near the Lord: but they shall not come nigh; neither shall the people go up with him.**

THE PROGRESSIVE CLIMB TO WORSHIP

And Moses came and told the people all the words of the Lord, and all the judgments: and all the people answered with one voice, and said, All the words which the Lord hath said will we do.

And Moses wrote all the words of the Lord, and rose up early in the morning, and builded an altar under the hill, and the twelve pillars, according to the twelve tribes of Israel.

And he sent young men of the children of Israel, which offered burnt-offerings, and sacrificed peace-offerings of oxen unto the Lord.

And Moses took half of the blood and put it in basons; and half of the blood he sprinkled on the altar.

And he took the book of the covenant, and read in the audience of the people: and they said, All that the Lord hath said will we do, and be obedient.

And Moses took the blood, and sprinkled it on the people, and said, Behold the blood of the covenant, which the Lord hath made with you concerning all these words.

Then went up Moses, and Aaron, Nadab, and Abihu, and seventy of the elders of Israel:

And they saw the God of Israel; and there was under his feet as it were a paved work of a sapphire stone, and as it were the body of heaven in his clearness.

And upon the nobles of the children of Israel he laid not his hand: also they saw God, and did eat and drink.

And the Lord said unto Moses, Come up to me into the mount, and be there: and I will give thee tables of stone, and a law, and commandments which I have written; that thou mayest teach them.

And Moses rose up, and his minister Joshua: and Moses went up into the mount of God.

And he said unto the elders, Tarry ye here for us, until we come again unto you: and, behold, Aaron and Hur are with you: if any man have any matters to do, let him come unto them.

THE MECHANICS OF TRUE WORSHIP

And Moses went up into the mount, and a cloud covered the mount.

And the glory of the Lord abode upon mount Sinai, and the cloud covered it six days: and the seventh day he called unto Moses out of the midst of the cloud.

And the sight of the glory of the Lord was like devouring fire on the top of the mount in the eyes of the children of Israel.

And Moses went into the midst of the cloud, and gat him up into the mount: and Moses was in the mount forty days and forty nights.

>Exodus 24:1-18

After God's appearance to Moses and the deliverance of the Israelites from slavery in Egypt, the foundation of Israelite ritual was laid. This type of worship took place in the light of history, especially the Exodus of the Hebrew people from Egypt. Through Moses, God established the form and principles of Israelite worship.

And the Lord spake unto Moses, saying,

Speak unto the children of Israel, that they bring me an offering: of every man that giveth it willingly with his heart ye shall take my offering.

And this is the offering which ye shall take of them; gold, and silver, and brass,

And blue, and purple, and scarlet, and fine linen, and goats' hair,

And rams' skins dyed red, and badgers' skins, and shittim wood,

Oil for the light, spices for anointing oil, and for sweet incense.

Onyx stones, and stones to be set in the ephod, and in the breastplate.

And let them make me a sanctuary; that I may dwell among them.

THE PROGRESSIVE CLIMB TO WORSHIP

According to all that I shew thee, after the pattern of the tabernacle, and the pattern of all the instruments thereof, even so shall ye make it.

Exodus 25:1-9

One key instruction that we see God giving Moses in the above Scripture was that those participating in the building of the tabernacle for worship were to be individuals that would bring offerings and possess a "willing heart" (verse 2). This is indicative of the nature of the heart of a true worshipper.

Every man of the children of Israel shall pitch by his own standard, with the ensign of their father's house: far off about the tabernacle of the congregation shall they pitch.
Numbers 2:2

This Scripture records the Lord's call for the tabernacle of the congregation to be situated in a strategic way among the twelve tribes.

God gave precise instruction for the tribes of Judah, Issachar and Zebulun to camp on the east side; the tribes of Ephraim, Mannaseh and Benjamin on the west. On the north side were to be Dan, Napthali and Asher; while remaining on the south side were Gad, Reuben and Simeon.

They then were to erect and place the tabernacle at the very center of these positionings. Only the sons of Aaron and the Levites could set up camp near the tabernacle. These were those set aside to minister unto God.

Like the hub of a bicycle wheel with its spokes radiating outward, this tribal arrangement around the tabernacle made some dramatic statements. "Let's keep worship at the center of life! Array the rest of your life around it."

However, the Israelites had to place their own personal tents far away from the tabernacle. The priests and Levites alone lived within close proximity. God allowed only those in the priesthood to enter into His very Presence.

THE MECHANICS OF TRUE WORSHIP

> And it came to pass, when Moses went out unto the tabernacle, that all the people rose up, and stood every man at his tent door, and looked after Moses, until he was gone into the tabernacle.
>
> And it came to pass, as Moses entered into the tabernacle, the cloudy pillar descended, and stood at the door of the tabernacle, and the Lord talked with Moses.
>
> And all the people saw the cloudy pillar stand at the tabernacle door: and all the people rose up and worshipped, every man in his tent door.
>
> **Exodus 33:8-10**

Being arrayed around the tabernacle did offer some advantages. One was that everyone could witness whenever Moses went in to meet with God.

After the occupation of the Promised Land, Israel's exposure to Canaanite worship affected the nation's own worship. The Old Testament reveals clearly that Israel adopted some of the practices of the pagan people around them. At various times, God's people lapsed into idolatry. Some idols were placed on pedestals and sometimes they were adorned or fastened with silver chains (Isaiah 40:19) or fastened with pegs lest they totter and fall (Isaiah 41:7). Shrines and altars were sometimes erected to these pagan gods. But such idolatry was condemned by God and His special spokesmen, the prophets of the Old Testament.

> But the hour cometh, and now is, when the true worshippers shall worship the Father in spirit and in truth: for the Father seeketh such to worship him.
>
> God is a Spirit; and they that worship him must worship him in spirit and in truth.
>
> **John 4:23-24**

> For we are the circumcision, which worship God in the spirit, and rejoice in Christ Jesus, and have no confidence in the flesh.
>
> **Philippians 3:3**

THE PROGRESSIVE CLIMB TO WORSHIP

Early New Testament worship was characterized by a joy and thanksgiving because of God's gracious redemption in Christ. This early Christian worship focused on God's saving work in Jesus Christ. True worship was that which occurred under the inspiration of God's Spirit.

> **And upon the first day of the week, when the disciples came together to break bread, Paul preached unto them, ready to depart on the morrow; and continued his speech until midnight**
>
> **Acts 20:7**

> **Upon the first day of the week let every one of you lay by him in store, as God hath prospered him, that there be no gatherings when I come.**
>
> **I Corinthians 16:2**

The Jewish Sabbath was quickly replaced by the first day of the week as the time for weekly public worship. This day soon became known as the Lord's Day.

> **I was in the Spirit on the Lord's day, and heard behind me a great voice, as of a trumpet,**
>
> **Revelations 1:10**

This was the occasion for celebration of the resurrection of Jesus since He arose on the first day of the week (Mark 16:2).

At first, worship services were conducted in private homes. Possibly for a time, the first Christians worshipped in the synagogues as well as private homes. Some scholars believe that the Jewish Christian would go to the synagogues on Saturdays and to their own meetings on Sundays.

Many early Christians of Jewish backgrounds continued to follow the law and customs of their people. They observed the Sabbath and the Jewish holy days, such as the great annual festivals. However, Apostle Paul held himself free from all such obligations and never held these obligations against those he converted (Col. 2:16). The New Testament itself contains no references to any yearly Christian festivals. The King James Version's mention of "Easter" in Acts 12:4 is a mistranslation; the New King James Version, the Amplified Version, the New International Version and the New American Standard Bible version all have "Passover."

Although the New Testament does not instruct worshippers in a specific procedure to follow in their services, several elements appear regularly in the worship practices of the Early Church:

PRAYER

Continue in prayer, and watch in the same with thanksgiving;

Colossians 4:2

Pray without ceasing.

I Thessalonians 5:17

Prayer apparently had a leading place in Christian worship. The letters of Apostle Paul regularly contained references to prayer for fellow believers in the faith. Prayer develops a humility in us all. Prayer will bring us to a realization that without God, we can do nothing. Prayer, therefore, is the bedrock of worship.

PRAISE

Praise also is key. Praise, either by individuals or in hymns sung in common, reflects the frequent use of psalms in the synagogue. Also, possible fragments of Christian hymns appear scattered through the New Testament.

And when they heard that, they lifted up their voice to God with one accord, and said, Lord, thou art God, which hast made heaven, and earth, and the sea, and all that in them is:

Who by the mouth of thy servant David hast said, Why did the heathen rage, and the people imagine vain things?

THE PROGRESSIVE CLIMB TO WORSHIP

The kings of the earth stood up, and the rulers were gathered together against the Lord, and against his Christ.

For of a truth against thy holy child Jesus, whom thou hast anointed, both Herod, and Pontius Pilate, with the Gentiles, and the people of Israel, were gathered together,

For to do whatsoever thy hand and thy counsel determined before to be done.

And now, Lord, behold their threatenings: and grant unto thy servants, that with all boldness they may speak thy word,

By stretching forth thine hand to heal; and that signs and wonders may be done by the name of thy holy child Jesus.

Acts 4:24-30

Wherefore he saith, Awake thou that sleepest, and arise from the dead, and Christ shall give thee light.

Ephesians 5:14

And without controversy great is the mystery of godliness: God was manifest in the flesh, justified in the Spirit, seen of angels, preached unto the Gentiles, believed on in the world, received up into glory.

I Timothy 3:16

And the four beasts had each of them six wings about him; and they were full of eyes within: and they rest not day and night, saying, Holy, holy, holy, Lord God Almighty, which was, and is, and is to come.

Thou art worthy, O Lord, to receive glory and honour and power: for thou hast created all things, and for thy pleasure they are and were created.

Revelation 4:8, 11

And they sung a new song, saying Thou art worthy to take the book, and to open the seals thereof: for thou wast slain, and hast redeemed us to God by thy blood out of every kindred, and tongue, and people, and nation;

And has made us unto our God kings and priests: and we shall reign on the earth.

Saying with a loud voice, Worthy is the Lamb that was slain to receive power, and riches, and wisdom, and strength, and honour, and glory, and blessing.

And every creature which is in heaven, and on the earth, and under the earth, and such as are in the sea, and all that are in them, heard I saying, Blessing, and honour, and glory, and power, be unto him that sitteth upon the throne, and unto the Lamb for ever and ever.

Revelations 5:9-10, 12, 13

Lessons from the Bible to be read and studied were another part of the worship procedure of the New Testament Church. Emphases were probably given to the messianic prophecies which had been fulfilled in Jesus Christ. His teachings also received a primary place.

Contributions were also collected on the first day of the week (I Cor. 16:2). Other details about the worship procedures of the early Christians in the New Testament times are spotty. But these elements must have been regularly included in the weekly worship service.

CHAPTER II

PREREQUISITES OF WORSHIP

The concept of worship is expressed by the term "serve." In general, the worship given to God was modeled after the service given to human sovereigns; this was especially prominent in pagan religions. In these the deities' image inhabited a palace (temple) and had servants (priests) who supplied food (offered sacrifices), washed and anointed and clothed, scented the air with incense, lit lamps at night, and guarded the doors to the house.

Worshippers brought offerings and tithes to the deity, said prayers and bowed down, as one might bring tribute and present petitions to a king. Indeed the very purpose of human existence in Mesopotamian thought was to provide the gods with the necessities of life.

Although Israelite worship shared many of the external forms of pagan worship, even to calling sacrifices the "food of God," its essence was quite different. God could not be worshipped only externally, but one's heartbeat had to be tied to the paying of this homage. Truly honoring God, it was necessary to obey His laws morally and ethically as well as those carried out ritually. To appear before God with sacrifices while flouting His demands for justice was to insult Him.

True worship must begin with a deeper look at the character of the worshipper. It is an established fact that we serve a holy God. But true worship does not stop at this fact. God Himself is also concerned with the condition of the vessel paying tribute to Him.

The concept of holiness has first of all been highly distorted. Holiness is not determined by one's outer appearance (clothes, hairstyle, make-up, etc.). Holiness is not even determined by one's outer projection of their own conduct or behavior. Holiness actually is derived from a word which denotes more of a concept of being "whole." Holy is the state of being whole, complete, being found in totality.

> They shall be holy unto their God, and not profane the name of their God: for the offerings of the LORD made by fire, and the bread of their God, they do offer: therefore they shall be holy.
>
> Leviticus 21:6

"HOLY UNTO THEIR GOD"

Now we begin to understand one of the first qualities that was a prerequisite in giving a genuine offering unto the Lord, in that the vessel is expected to be "holy" — complete, whole. Thank God it did not ask for those that were perfect, but for those that were holy. A wholeness can be achieved in one's heart, attitude and motives toward God without being perfect. Submitting totally unto God allows Him to make us holy.

Therefore, a prerequisite of the scripture "they shall be holy unto their God ..." can be achieved by allowing God to make us holy.

> And thou shalt make a plate of pure gold, and grave upon it, like the engravings of a signet, HOLINESS TO THE LORD.
>
> Exodus 28:36

> And I will sanctify the tabernacle of the congregation, and the altar: I will sanctify also both Aaron and his sons, to minister to me in the priest's office.
>
> Exodus 29:44

> Then Moses said unto Aaron, This is it that the LORD spake, saying, I will be sanctified in them that come nigh me, and before all the people I will be glorified. And Aaron held his peace.
>
> Leviticus 10:3

> Thou shalt sanctify him therefore; for he offereth the bread of thy God: he shall be holy unto thee: for I the LORD, which sanctify you, am holy.
>
> Leviticus 21:8

> And I said unto them, Ye are holy unto the LORD; the vessels are holy also; and the silver and the gold are a freewill offering unto the LORD God of your fathers.
>
> Ezra 8:28

> But ye are a chosen generation, a royal priesthood, an holy nation, a peculiar people; that ye should shew forth the praises of him who hath called you out of darkness into his marvellous light:
>
> I Peter 2:9

"NOT PROFANING THE NAME OF GOD"

Another requirement of the vessel worshipping God was that the vessel itself could not profane God's Holy Name. In the Old Testament, the Hebrew word for profane was "chalal." This holds a powerful connotation in that it is saying that the vessel worshipping God must never "pollute, stain, prostitute" or even "wound" the Name of God. How can we do this? By not taming the tongue. We must control our mouths. Our speech, especially concerning the Name of the Lord, must always be of a positive nature. But how can we guarantee that our mouths never fall guilty to profaning God? A good way is by knowing just who He is!

A.J. Tozer has said that our most important thought is our conception of God. It should be as close as possible to the truth. Only then can we "worship Him in spirit and in truth." It's critical that we grasp as much as we can about the One who created us, loves us and died for us, and waits for the fulfillment of all things. John gave us a peek at the future, so let's gaze back at the past— which, of course, is all the same to God.

We can uncover a wealth of insight into the nature of God by looking at His different names. In the Hebrew language a name held much more significance than in English today. It expressed the nature, character or purpose of that which it named. To pursue our understanding of who God is, we can best begin with how He revealed Himself to the children of Israel.

ELOHIM

In the first verse of the first chapter of the book of the Bible, we've all read or heard *God created ...* The Word of God here is *Elohim*, and in it reside the first clues to God's identity. Elohim, a plural word, indicates His triune nature and His supremacy as the Creator. The One we worship is the *Eternal, Immortal, Invisible, The Only Wise God.* (I Timothy 1:17). He is the Father, Son and Holy Spirit, as well as *our* Father, *our* Lord, and the Spirit living in every believer.

God is eternal, and therefore, not bound by the restrictions of time. He exists outside of time itself. As the Apostle Peter noted, a thousand years may be as one day in His sight. Space cannot bind Him either. In His omnipresence and omniscience, He is present always and everywhere. He sees and knows all things.

On only one occasion has God limited Himself to the boundaries of time, and He did that for us! He chose to become a man. He decided to become part of His creation in order to rescue it. When Jesus came in the flesh, He lived under the same rules He expected man to obey. Then the Lord went one step further. He submitted Himself to His own invention and allowed it to crucify Him.

God expressed His divinity through creation, but He is much greater than anything in it. He is set apart. Elohim created all and controls all, yet remains as separate from His creation as an artist from his painting. A painting on canvas is but a reflection of the artist, not the artist himself. So does the universe only reflect Elohim.

When we speak of the activity of God, we refer to the Creator as we see Him in the opening chapters of Genesis and the first chapter of John. Our Lord Jesus (the Word) certainly demonstrated an active part of the Trinity.

In the beginning was the Word, and the Word was with God, and the Word was God.

He was in the beginning with God.

All things came into being by Him; and apart from Him nothing came into being that has come into being.

John 1:1-3 (NASB)

Let's worship Him, the eternal Creator, Elohim!

EL SHADDAI

This name appears in Genesis 17:1 as God's declaration to Abram. "I am El Shaddai: Almighty God." God's name combined His great and glorious nature (El) with His ability to provide (Shaddai). The meaning of Shaddai comes close to "a mother's breast." In the same way that a mother's breast nourishes, comforts, and satisfied a helpless baby, so does our God do for us. In comparison to the vast universe, we are helpless.

We might add that only after God declared Himself as El Shaddai, did He establish the covenant with Abram and change his name to Abraham. God was stating His intent and ability to fulfill His part in the relationship with Abraham and all of his descendants. Up until that time, people knew God as the Creator in an impersonal sort of way, but with this covenant things changed. God unveiled a new revelation of His nature and a unique relationship began.

Let's worship Him, Almighty God, El Shaddai!

JEHOVAH-JIREH

The meaning of this name occurs in the passage where God commanded Abraham to offer his precious, long-awaited son as a sacrifice. The Lord required such obedience from Abraham as a means of testing or proving his faithfulness. Abraham needed to learn to trust God implicitly. Would God provide a means for his son Isaac to return with him from the mountain? Abraham believed so. His words to his servants even before climbing the mount of sacrifice showed his faith.

> On the third day Abraham raised his eyes and saw the place from a distance. And Abraham said unto his young men,
>
> "Stay here with the donkey, and I and the lad will go yonder; and we will worship and return to you."
> Genesis 22:4-5 (NASB)

Abraham's confidence in El Shaddai never wavered. He may not have known the details of how Isaac would survive, but he knew that God would be faithful to His earlier promises. As we read further on, God demonstrated His undisputed authority. All He required? Abraham's unquestioning obedience,

> And Abraham stretched out his hand, and took the knife to slay his son.
>
> But the angel of the Lord called to him from heaven, and said, "Abraham, Abraham!" And he said, Here I am.
>
> And he said, "Do not stretch out your hand against the lad, and do nothing to him; for now I know that you fear God, since you have not withheld your son, your only son, from Me."
>
> Then Abraham raised his eyes and looked, and behold, behind him a ram caught in the thicket by his horns; and Abraham went and took the ram, and offered him up for a burnt offering in the place of his son.
>
> And Abraham called the name of that place (Jehovah-jireh), the Lord will provide, as it is said to this day, "In the mount of the Lord it will be provided."
>
> Genesis 22:10-14 (NASB)

Abraham's tremendous act of faith foreshadowed the day when another Father would offer His only Son. Only He wouldn't spare His life—on purpose. Let's worship Him, the Lord our provider, Jehovah-jireh!

PREREQUISITES OF WORSHIP

JEHOVAH-NISSI

The name means "the Lord our banner," the One high above us and around whom we rally in difficult times. He goes ahead of us in battle (spiritual and natural) so we know which direction to travel. When we look up at Him, He boosts our confidence and bolsters our courage so we can keep fighting to the end.

After their miraculous deliverance from Egypt, the children of Israel confronted the Amalekite tribe. In this first battle, God revealed Himself as Jehovah-nissi through Moses.

> So Moses said to Joshua, "Choose men for us, and go out, fight against Amalek. Tomorrow I will station myself on the top of the hill with the staff of God in my hand."
>
> And Joshua did as Moses told him, and fought against Amalek; and Moses, Aaron, and Hur went up to the top of the hill.
>
> So it came about when Moses held his hand up that Israel prevailed, and when he let his hand down, Amalek prevailed.
>
> But Moses' hands were heavy. Then they took a stone and put it under him, and he sat on it; and Aaron and Hur supported his hands, one on one side and one on the other. Thus his hands were steady until the sun set.
>
> So Joshua overwhelmed Amalek and his people with the edge of the sword. Then the Lord said to Moses, Write this in a book as a memorial, and recite it to Joshua, that I will utterly blot out the memory of Amalek from under heaven.
> And Moses built an altar; and named it (Jehovah-nissi) the Lord is my banner.
>
> Exodus 17:9-15 (NASB)

Each time Moses held up the rod of God the people gained enough strength to overcome the enemy. When the rod came down they lost ground. This rod, then, provided a visible standard or ensign around which the people rallied, and when it remained high in the air, God performed feats of victory. Symbolic of God Himself, the rod pointed forward through the ages to Jesus.

Like Moses, who built an altar to commemorate the Lord's Name and His role in battle, we might remind ourselves often of the One high above us. We gather around Jehovah-nissi and exalt Him who *always causes us to triumph* (I Corinthians 2:14).

Let's worship Him, the Lord our banner, Jehovah-nissi!

JEHOVAH-ROPHE

After the children of Israel crossed the Red Sea by a mighty miracle, they languished in the wilderness without water for three days. When they finally found water it was too bitter to drink. What disappointment! Once again, God proved He was truly their provider. Through the miraculous, He confirmed this new revelation of His nature as their healer, Jehovah-rophe,

> **So the people grumbled at Moses saying, "What shall we drink?"**
>
> **Then he cried out to the Lord, and the Lord showed him a tree; and he threw it into the waters, and the waters became sweet. There He made for them a statute and regulation, and there He tested them.**
>
> **And He said, "If you will give earnest heed to the voice of the Lord your God, and do what is right in His sight, and give ear to His commandments, and keep all His statutes, I will put none of the diseases on you which I put on the Egyptians; for I, the Lord, am (Jehovah-rophe) your healer."**
>
> Exodus 15:24-26 (NASB)

Let's worship Him, the Lord our healer, Jehovah-rophe!

JEHOVAH-SHALOM

This name means "the Lord our peace." We could use a calming hand upon us during these troubled times. Gideon met God as Jehovah-shalom at a crucial point in his life and in history. The people of Israel were enduring extreme hardship under the oppressive power of the Midianites. They cried out for deliverance. God responded to their plea by sending an angel to tell Gideon he had been chosen to be the instrument of their release.

Skepticism and fear gripped Gideon's heart. He didn't feel up to the dangerous task and reminded the Lord why. He came from the poorest, weakest clan and he was the weakest among them, no less. That didn't bother God. He told Gideon He would be with him. Gideon offered a present to the Lord of bread and meat and said he needed a more dramatic assurance of God's favor. He got it. With a touch of the angel's staff to the rock, fire sprang up and consumed Gideon's offering. But then he felt more afraid than ever.

When Gideon saw that he was an angel of the Lord, he said, "Alas, O Lord God! For now I have seen the angel of the Lord face to face."

And the Lord said to him, "Peace to you, do not fear; you shall not die." Then Gideon built an altar there to the Lord and named it (Jehovah-shalom) the Lord is peace.
                                                Judges 6:22-24 (NASB)

This revelation came at a time of national unrest and in the face of insurmountable odds. The same holds true for us today. No matter what circumstances we face ... despite how things look, or how we feel in the midst of turmoil ... we have a wonderful assurance. Our peace does not depend upon anyone or anything. God is our peace.

Let's worship Him, the Lord our peace, Jehovah-shalom!

JEHOVAH-TSIDKENU

All our own righteous deeds are as filthy rags before a holy God, the Word reminds us in Isaiah 64:6. We need something outside ourselves to make us clean. God gave us this name, "the Lord our righteousness," in a prophetic word to Jeremiah.

> "Behold the days are coming," declares the Lord, "when I will raise up for David a righteous Branch, and he will reign as king and act wisely, and do justice and righteousness in the land."
>
> In His days Judah will be saved, and Israel will dwell securely; and this is His name by which he will be called, (Jehovah-tsidkenu) The Lord our righteousness.
>
> Jeremiah 23:5-6 (NASB)

Jehovah-tsidkenu points forward to the coming of Jesus as the perfect Lamb of God. We find in the writing of the Apostle Paul that Jesus, who knew no sin, took on the burden of sin so that we might become the righteousness of God in Him (II Corinthians 5:21). In a kind of divine exchange, we give Him our sin; He gives us His holiness. We turn in our old, dirty clothes; He dresses us in a brand new set of white garments.

Let's worship Him, the Lord our righteousness, Jehovah-tsidkenu!

JEHOVAH-M'KADDESH

Here we find another facet of God's nature, later manifested in the Son of God— Jehovah-m'kaddesh, the Lord our sanctifier. In addition to washing us clean inwardly (righteousness), He sets us apart as a unique, holy people of His own. His purposes become ours, and He uses us as He sees fit. In the Old Testament, keeping one day of the week as a special "Lord's day" provided an outward demonstration of His people's uniqueness. God gave the commandment to Moses,

> But as for you, speak to the sons of Israel, saying, You shall surely observe My sabbaths; for this is a sign between Me and you throughout your generations, that you may know that I am (Jehovah-m'kaddesh) the Lord who sanctifies you.
>
> Exodus 31:13 (NASB)

JEHOVAH-SHAMMAH

God revealed Himself to Ezekiel as Jehovah-shammah, the One who is always present. The prophet had a vision of the Holy City the Lord will establish upon the new earth at the close of the age. New Jerusalem will be God's dwelling place forever, *The city shall be 18,000 cubits round about; and the name of the city from that day shall be (Jehovah-shammah), the Lord is there.*

This passage does speak of a future event, but applies to us today, as well. God still meets with man in His tabernacle or temple. We, the members of His body, are living temples in which His Holy Spirit dwells (I Corinthians 3:16). Jesus promised in Matthew 28:20, ... lo, **I am with you always,** even to the end of the age. On that glorious day we will walk the streets of New Jerusalem and see God face to face.

Let's worship Him, the Lord who is ever present with us, Jehovah-shammah!

JEHOVAH-ROHI

Almost everyone knows the beautiful psalm of King David: *The Lord is my shepherd; I shall not want* ... (Psalm 23:1). Jesus reminds us of the identity of the tender-hearted shepherd and how we can recognize Him,

> **I am the good shepherd: the good shepherd lays down his life for the sheep.**
>
> **He who is a hireling, and not a shepherd, who is not the owner of the sheep, beholds the wolf coming, and leaves the sheep, and flees, and the wolf snatches them, and scatters them.**
>
> **John 10:11-12 (NASB)**

Without a leader to follow, we wander astray as easily as simple-minded sheep. They don't even know when they're lost. Our watchful, gentle Shepherd leads us to quiet waters of His Holy Spirit where we quench our thirst and to rich pastures of His Word where He guards us as we eat our fill. In that beautiful spot, He binds up our wounds and pursues us if we should wander off. He heals our broken hearts and leads us down paths of blessing because His name is at stake. When He makes a promise, He keeps it.

Let's worship Him, our good shepherd, Jehovah-rohi!

JEHOVAH-ELYON

This name elevates God as the Lord Most High. There is none higher than He! *For the Lord Most High is to be feared, a great King over all the earth; Thou art exalted far above all gods* (Psalm 97:9).

Let's worship Him, the Lord Most High, Jehovah-elyon!

JEHOVAH-HOSEENU

Jehovah-hoseenu is the Lord our Maker, our personal Creator with whom we have a covenant relationship. This name acknowledges God as more than just the Creator of nature and other living things. He has a right to us as well— our time, talent, treasure and thoughts. *Come, let us worship and bow down; Let us kneel before the Lord our Maker* (Psalm 95:6).

Let's worship Him, the Lord our Maker, Jehovah-hoseenu!

JEHOVAH-ELOHEENU

In this name God declares Himself as the Lord our God. He is both Lord and a holy, set-apart God only to those of us who have entered into a covenant with Him.

PREREQUISITES OF WORSHIP

Exalt the Lord our God, and worship at His footstool; Holy is He ...
O Lord our God, Thou didst answer them; Thou wast a forgiving God to them, and yet an avenger of their evil deeds.

Exalt the Lord our God, and worship at His holy hill, for holy is the Lord our God.
Psalm 99:5, 8-9 (NASB)

Let's worship Him, the Lord our God, Jehovah-eloheenu!

JEHOVAH-ELOHIM

We find the first of many occurrences of this title, the Lord God, in the second chapter of Genesis, *These are the generations of the heavens and of the earth when they were created, in the day that the Lord God made the earth and the heaven* (Genesis 2:4). This name, like others, proclaims the Self-Existent One, the Eternal Creator of all things, in covenant relationship with His people.

Let's worship Him, the Lord God, Jehovah-elohim!

JEHOVAH-ELOHEKA

When God gave Moses the ten commandments, He said He was Jehovah-eloheka, Israel's Lord,

I am the Lord your God, who brought you out of the land of Egypt, out of the house of slavery ...

You shall not worship them or serve them; for I, the Lord your God, am a jealous God ...

You shall not take the name of the Lord your God in vain.

Exodus 20:2, 5, 7 (NASB)

Worship Him spiritual Israel— the Lord your God, Jehovah-eloheka!

JEHOVAH-ELOHAY

God reveals Himself in even more of a personal relationship with His people. Each individual who knows Him can call Him "The Lord my God," the One who cares about me, no matter what events take place in the world. The prophet Zechariah referred to Him as such,

> ... Then the Lord, my God, will come, and all the holy ones with Him!
>
> And it will come about in that day that there will be no light; the luminaries will dwindle.
>
> For it will be a unique day which is known to the Lord, neither day nor night, but it will come about that at evening time there will be light.
>
> And the Lord will be king over all the earth; in that day the Lord will be the only one, and His name the only one.
>
> Zechariah 14:5-7, 9 (NASB)

Let each of us worship Him, the Lord my God, Jehovah-elohay!

JEHOVAH-SABAOTH

Perhaps the most famous passage in the Old Testament recounts the story of David and Goliath. It contains further revelation of God's character as Jehovah-sabaoth, the Lord of heaven's entire army of spiritual beings. You remember the scenario. An arrogant Philistine giant, Goliath, had been taunting the Israelite army over and over, until finally a champion emerged—the young shepherd boy. But this unlikely warrior candidate knew his God. He had depended on Him when he faced wild animals who threatened his sheep. David ventured forth, not with the cumbersome, unfamiliar weapons of Saul's army, but with his faithful staff and sling. Watch the thrilling encounter,

PREREQUISITES OF WORSHIP

> And the Philistine said to David, "Am I a dog, that you come to me with sticks?" And the Philistine cursed David by his gods.
>
> The Philistine also said to David, "Come to me, and I will give your flesh to the birds of the sky and the beasts of the field."
>
> Then David said to the Philistine, You come to me with a sword, a spear, and a javelin, but I come to you in the name of the Lord of Hosts (Jehovah-sabaoth), the God of the armies of Israel, whom you have taunted.
>
> I Samuel 17:43-45 (NASB)

David charged and defeated Israel's intimidating enemy because he knew the name of his power source. He advanced in the strength of the God he served. We, too, can defeat every "giant" in the powerful name of the Lord— by His authority.

Let's worship Him, the Lord of hosts, Jehovah-sabaoth!

There are many more redemptive names of God but these should at least begin to give us a clue to who God really is, so we can speak on these things and exalt His Name rather than profess it.

> And thou shalt not let any of thy seed pass through the fire to Molech, neither shalt thou profane the name of thy God: I am the LORD.
>
> Leviticus 18:21

> And ye shall not swear by my name falsely, neither shalt thou profane the name of thy God: I am the LORD.
>
> Leviticus 19:12

> A son honoureth his father, and a servant his master: if then I be a father, where is mine honour? and if I be a master, where is my fear? saith the LORD of hosts unto you, O priests, that despise my name. And ye say, Wherein have we despised thy name?
>
> Malachi 1:6

For from the rising of the sun even unto the going down of the same my name shall be great among the Gentiles; and in every place incense shall be offered unto my name, and a pure offering: for my name shall be great among the heathen, saith the LORD of hosts.

But ye have profaned it, in that ye say, The table of the LORD is polluted; and the fruit thereof, even his meat, is contemptible.

Malachi 1:11-12

Depart ye, depart ye, go ye out from thence, touch no unclean *thing*; go ye out of the midst of her; be ye clean, that bear the vessels of the Lord.

Isaiah 52:11

"BE YE CLEAN"

Another prerequisite of true worship is a state of being clean. In today's church, we are not speaking of a physical cleanliness of hands, feet and face (even though these things are expected), but a cleanliness of heart. This cleanliness symbolically speaks about dealing with unconfessed sin. We must always remember the act of repentance before entering into a mode of worship.

Depart ye, depart ye, go ye out from thence, touch no unclean thing; go ye out of the midst of her; be ye clean, that bear the vessels of the LORD.

Isaiah 52:11

Then Moses said unto Aaron, This is it that the LORD spake, saying, I will be sanctified in them that come nigh me, and before all the people I will be glorified. And Aaron held his peace.

Leviticus 10:3

Speak unto Aaron and to his sons, that they separate themselves from the holy things of the children of Israel, and that they profane not my holy name in those things which they hallow unto me: I am the LORD.

PREREQUISITES OF WORSHIP

Say unto them, Whosoever he be of all your seed among your generations, that goeth unto the holy things, which the children of Israel hallow unto the LORD, having his uncleanness upon him, that soul shall be cut off from my presence: I am the LORD.

What man soever of the seed of Aaron is a leper, or hath a running issue; he shall not eat of the holy things, until he be clean. And whoso toucheth any thing that is unclean by the dead, or a man whose seed goeth from him;

Or whosoever toucheth any creeping thing, whereby he may be made unclean, or a man of whom he may take uncleanness, whatsoever uncleanness he hath;

The soul which hath touched any such shall be unclean until even, and shall not eat of the holy things, unless he wash his flesh with water.

And when the sun is down, he shall be clean, and shall afterward eat of the holy things; because it is his food.

That which dieth of itself, or is torn with beasts, he shall not eat to defile himself therewith: I am the LORD.

They shall therefore keep mine ordinance, lest they bear sin for it, and die therefore, if they profane it: I the LORD do sanctify them.

There shall no stranger eat of the holy thing: a sojourner of the priest, or an hired servant, shall not eat of the holy thing.

But if the priest buy any soul with his money, he shall eat of it, and he that is born in his house: they shall eat of his meat.

If the priest's daughter also be married unto a stranger, she may not eat of an offering of the holy things.

But if the priest's daughter be a widow, or divorced, and have no child, and is returned unto her father's house, as in her youth, she shall eat of her father's meat: but there shall no stranger eat thereof.

And if a man eat of the holy thing unwittingly, then he shall put the fifth part thereof unto it, and shall give it unto the priest with the holy thing.

And they shall not profane the holy things of the children of Israel, which they offer unto the LORD;

Or suffer them to bear the iniquity of trespass, when they eat their holy things: for I the LORD do sanctify them.

And the LORD spake unto Moses, saying,

Speak unto Aaron, and to his sons, and unto all the children of Israel, and say unto them, Whatsoever he be of the house of Israel, or of the strangers in Israel, that will offer his oblation for all his vows, and for all his freewill offerings, which they will offer unto the LORD for a burnt offering;

Ye shall offer at your own will a male without blemish, of the beeves, of the sheep, or of the goats.

But whatsoever hath a blemish, that shall ye not offer: for it shall not be acceptable for you.

And whosoever offereth a sacrifice of peace offerings unto the LORD to accomplish his vow, or a freewill offering in beeves or sheep, it shall be perfect to be accepted; there shall be no blemish therein.

Blind, or broken, or maimed, or having a wen, or scurvy, or scabbed, ye shall not offer these unto the LORD, nor make an offering by fire of them upon the altar unto the LORD.

Either a bullock or a lamb that hath any thing superfluous or lacking in his parts, that mayest thou offer for a freewill offering; but for a vow it shall not be accepted.

Ye shall not offer unto the LORD that which is bruised, or crushed, or broken, or cut; neither shall ye make any offering thereof in your land.

Neither from a stranger's hand shall ye offer the bread of your God of any of these; because their corruption is in them, and blemishes be in them: they shall not be accepted for you.

And the LORD spake unto Moses, saying,

When a bullock, or a sheep, or a goat, is brought forth, then it shall be seven days under the dam; and from the eighth day and thenceforth it shall be accepted for an offering made by fire unto the LORD.

And whether it be cow or ewe, ye shall not kill it and her young both in one day.

PREREQUISITES OF WORSHIP

And when ye will offer a sacrifice of thanksgiving unto the LORD, offer it at your own will.

On the same day it shall be eaten up; ye shall leave none of it until the morrow: I am the LORD.

Therefore shall ye keep my commandments, and do them: I am the LORD.

Neither shall ye profane my holy name; but I will be hallowed among the children of Israel: I am the LORD which hallow you,

That brought you out of the land of Egypt, to be your God: I am the LORD.

           Leviticus 22:2-33

We see quite clearly here that it was quite involved to maintain this type of cleanliness. But because of the work of Christ, we have a better covenant. We still must remain clean but the means is different. We must confess all sin, repent and receive God's forgiveness.

CHAPTER III

SACRIFICES, OFFERINGS & RITUALS

We saw in a previous chapter that the Israelites had come to a point of external worship of God only. They were great doers of ritualistic laws (both moral and ethical). God then, and still is now, looking for more of a personal relationship. He is demanding an internal worship, a worship of the heart.

In the following Scriptures, we see that God rejected and despised the sacrificial offerings of the children of Israel. God certainly did not need the sacrifices given (Psalm 50:12-13); but the sacrifices and other forms of worship were offered to honor God as King.

> To what purpose is the multitude of your sacrifices unto me? Saith the LORD: I am full of the burnt offerings of rams, and the fat of fed beasts; and I delight not in the blood of bullocks, or of lambs, or of he goats.
>
> When ye come to appear before me, who hath required this at your hand, to tread my courts?
>
> Bring no more vain oblations; incense is an abomination unto me; the new moons and sabbaths, the calling of assemblies, I cannot away with; it is iniquity, even the solemn meeting.
>
> Your new moons and your appointed feasts my soul hateth: they are a trouble unto me; I am weary to bear them.
>
> And when ye spread forth your hands, I will hide mine eyes from you: yea, when ye make many prayers, I will not hear: your hands are full of blood. Wash you, make you clean; put away the evil of your doings from before mine eyes; cease to do evil;
>
> Learn to do well; seek judgment, relieve the oppressed, judge the fatherless, plead for the widow.
>
> Isaiah 1:11-17

> I hate, I reject your festivals, nor do I delight in your solemn assemblies. Even though you offer up to Me burnt offerings and your grain offerings, I will not accept them; and I will not even look at the peace offerings of your fatlings.
>
> Amos 5:21-22 (NASB)

Ideal Israelite worship is depicted in the priestly instructions of Exodus, Leviticus and Numbers. Its most prominent feature was sacrifice. Sacrifices were brought as gifts to God. Sacrifices or offerings were common practices in the Old Testament.

The most important part of any animal sacrifice was the disposal of the blood at the altar. Whether dashed against its sides, or smeared on its horns, the ritual act made the sacrifice valid; in fact, it distinguished sacrifice from mere slaughter. In addition, the blood of the sin and guilt offerings was used to cleanse the sanctuary.

> **What man soever there be of the house of Israel, that killeth an ox, or lamb, or goat, in the camp, or that killeth it out of the camp,**
>
> **And bringeth it not unto the door of the tabernacle of the congregation, to offer an offering unto the LORD before the tabernacle of the LORD; blood shall be imputed unto that man; he hath shed blood; and that man shall be cut off from among his people**
>
> **Leviticus 17:3-4**

This Scripture reveals that the Levitical laws required all animals eligible as offerings to be sacrificed, rather than simply slaughtered.

Priestly Roles

The priest was the one to officiate at the altar. Therefore, it was the priest that had to carry out the following:

THE BURNING OF THE ANIMALS SUET. The animal's suet (the hard fat on the entrails) and kidney belonged to God and therefore had to be burned on the altar.

> **And Aaron's sons shall burn it on the altar upon the burnt sacrifice, which is upon the wood that is on the fire: it is an offering made by fire, of a sweet savour unto the LORD.**

SACRIFICES, OFFERINGS & RITUALS

> And the priest shall burn it upon the altar: it is the food of the offering made by fire unto the LORD.
>
> And the priest shall burn them upon the altar: it is the food of the offering made by fire for a sweet savour: all the fat is the LORD'S.
>
> **Leviticus 3:5, 11, 16**

THE RECEIVING OF CHOICE OFFERINGS. In exchange for his services, the priest received some portion of the sacrifice. Cattle, sheep, goats, doves and pigeons were the only kinds of animals that could be offered, and vegetable offerings used wheat, barley, olive oil, wine and frankincense.

THE SALTING OF ALL OFFERINGS. The priest had to make sure that all of the choice offerings were seasoned with salt.

> Every grain offering of yours, moreover, you shall season with salt, so that the salt of the covenant of your God shall not be lacking from your grain offering; with all your offerings you shall offer salt.
>
> **Leviticus 2:13**

> And thou shalt offer them before the LORD, and the priests shall cast salt upon them, and they shall offer them up for a burnt offering unto the LORD.
>
> **Ezekiel 43:24**

OVERSEEING THE PHYSICAL CONDITION OF THE OFFERINGS. The sacrificial animals had to be unblemished; that is, they could not be diseased or injured or castrated.

> And the LORD spake unto Moses, saying,
>
> Speak unto Aaron, and to his sons, and unto all the children of Israel, and say unto them, Whatsoever he be of the house of Israel, or of the strangers in Israel, that will offer his oblation for all his vows, and for all his freewill offerings, which they will offer unto the LORD for a burnt offering;

> Ye shall offer at your own will a male without blemish, of the beeves, of the sheep, or of the goats.
>
> But whatsoever hath a blemish, that shall ye not offer: for it shall not be acceptable for you.
>
> And whosoever offereth a sacrifice of peace offerings unto the LORD to accomplish his vow, or a freewill offering in beeves or sheep, it shall be perfect to be accepted; there shall be no blemish therein.
>
> Blind, or broken, or maimed, or having a wen, or scurvy, or scabbed, ye shall not offer these unto the LORD, nor make an offering by fire of them upon the altar unto the LORD.
>
> Either a bullock or a lamb that hath any thing superfluous or lacking in his parts, that mayest thou offer for a freewill offering; but for a vow it shall not be accepted.
>
> Ye shall not offer unto the LORD that which is bruised, or crushed, or broken, or cut; neither shall ye make any offering thereof in your land.
>
> Neither from a stranger's hand shall ye offer the bread of your God of any of these; because their corruption is in them, and blemishes be in them: they shall not be accepted for you.
>
> Leviticus 22:17-25

Different Types of Offerings

BURNT OFFERING. The burnt offering (Lev. 1) was the commonest and most general sacrifice. Appropriate for atonement or thanksgiving, its purpose, basically, was to win God's favor. It was probably the oldest kind of sacrifice (mentioned throughout the Bible) and played a major role in public worship (Numbers 28-29) and rites of cleansing (Leviticus 12:6, 8; 14:19,22; 15:15, 30; 16:24). The animals offered had to be male (except birds). The animal was entirely burned on the altar, except for the hide, which went to the priest.

SACRIFICES, OFFERINGS & RITUALS

> Also the priest who presents any man's burnt offering, that priest shall have for himself the skin of the burnt offering which he has presented.
>
> Leviticus 7:8 (NASB)

PEACE OFFERING. The peace offering (Leviticus 3) was brought when one wished to eat meat. It could be a bull or a cow, or a sheep or a goat (male or female). The officiating priest received the right thigh, while the animal's breast was shared by all the priests.

> And the priest shall burn the fat upon the altar: but the breast shall be Aaron's and his sons'.
>
> And the right shoulder shall ye give unto the priest for an heave offering of the sacrifices of your peace offerings.
>
> He among the sons of Aaron, that offereth the blood of the peace offerings, and the fat, shall have the right shoulder for his part.
>
> For the wave breast and the heave shoulder have I taken of the children of Israel from off the sacrifices of their peace offerings, and have given them unto Aaron the priest and unto his sons by a statute for ever from among the children of Israel.
>
> Leviticus 7:31-34

The person bringing the sacrifice received the rest of the animal, which had to be eaten within one or two days.

> And the flesh of the sacrifice of his peace offerings for thanksgiving shall be eaten the same day that it is offered; he shall not leave any of it until the morning.
>
> Leviticus 7:15

> It shall be eaten the same day ye offer it, and on the morrow: and if ought remain until the third day, it shall be burnt in the fire.
>
> And if it be eaten at all on the third day, it is abominable; it shall not be accepted.

> Therefore every one that eateth it shall bear his iniquity, because he hath profaned the hallowed thing of the LORD: and that soul shall be cut off from among his people.
>
> Leviticus 19:6-8

The peace offering was further subdivided, according to purpose, into the thanksgiving offering, free-will offering, and votive offering.

> And this is the law of the sacrifice of peace offerings, which he shall offer unto the LORD.
>
> If he offer it for a thanksgiving, then he shall offer with the sacrifice of thanksgiving unleavened cakes mingled with oil, and unleavened wafers anointed with oil, and cakes mingled with oil, of fine flour, fried.
>
> Besides the cakes, he shall offer for his offering leavened bread with the sacrifice of thanksgiving of his peace offerings.
>
> And of it he shall offer one out of the whole oblation for an heave offering unto the LORD, and it shall be the priest's that sprinkleth the blood of the peace offerings.
>
> And the flesh of the sacrifice of his peace offerings for thanksgiving shall be eaten the same day that it is offered; he shall not leave any of it until the morning.
>
> But if the sacrifice of his offering be a vow, or a voluntary offering, it shall be eaten the same day that he offereth his sacrifice: and on the morrow also the remainder of it shall be eaten:
>
> But the remainder of the flesh of the sacrifice on the third day shall be burnt with fire.
>
> And if any of the flesh of the sacrifice of his peace offerings be eaten at all on the third day, it shall not be accepted, neither shall it be imputed unto him that offereth it: it shall be an abomination, and the soul that eateth of it shall bear his iniquity.
>
> Leviticus 7:11-18

SACRIFICES, OFFERINGS & RITUALS

Psalm 107 mentions four occasions for which a thanksgiving offering would be appropriate: successful passage through the desert, release from prison, recovery from a serious illness, or surviving a storm at sea. The votive offering was given to repay a vow,

> And it came to pass after forty years, that Absalom said unto the king, I pray thee, let me go and pay my vow, which I have vowed unto the LORD, in Hebron.
>
> For thy servant vowed a vow while I abode at Geshur in Syria, saying, If the LORD shall bring me again indeed to Jerusalem, then I will serve the LORD.
>
> II Samuel 15:7-8

while the free-will offering needed no special occasion. These offerings were distinguished ritually, in that the thanksgiving offering required different kinds of accompaniment and had to be eaten in one day, whereas the votive offering and the free-will offering could be left over one night and finished on the following day. Under no circumstances could a sacrifice be eaten after the second day.

> If he offers it by way of thanksgiving, then along with the sacrifice of thanksgiving he shall offer unleavened cakes mixed with oil, and unleavened wafers spread with oil, and cakes of well stirred fine flour mixed with oil.
>
> Leviticus 7:12 (NASB)

> And the flesh of the sacrifice of his peace offerings for thanksgiving shall be eaten the same day that it is offered; he shall not leave any of it until the morning.
>
> But if the sacrifice of his offering be a vow, or a voluntary offering, it shall be eaten the same day that he offereth his sacrifice: and on the morrow also the remainder of it shall be eaten:
>
> But the remainder of the flesh of the sacrifice on the third day shall be burnt with fire.

> And if any of the flesh of the sacrifice of his peace offerings be eaten at all on the third day, it shall not be accepted, neither shall it be imputed unto him that offereth it: it shall be an abomination, and the soul that eateth of it shall bear his iniquity.
>
> Leviticus 7:15-18

ORDINATION OFFERING. The ordination offering was a special type of peace offering whose blood was used as part of the ritual ordaining the high priest. Like the thanksgiving offering, it had a bread accompaniment and had to be eaten on the same day that it was offered.

> **Then you shall take the other ram, and Aaron and his sons shall lay their hands on the head of the ram.**
>
> **And you shall slaughter the ram, and take some of its blood and put it on the lobe of Aaron's right ear and on the lobes of his sons' right ears and on the thumbs of their right hands and on the big toes of their right feet, and sprinkle the rest of the blood around on the altar.**
>
> **Then you shall take some of the blood that is on the altar and some of the anointing oil, and sprinkle it on Aaron and on his garments, and on his sons and on his sons' garments with him; so he and his garments shall be consecrated, as well as his sons and his sons' garments with him.**
>
> **You shall also take the fat from the ram and the fat tail, and the fat that covers the entrails and the lobe of the liver, and the two kidneys and the fat that is on them and the right thigh (for it is a ram of ordination),**
>
> **and one cake of bread and one cake of bread mixed with oil and one wafer from the basket of unleavened bread which is set before the Lord;**
>
> **and you shall put all these in the hands of Aaron and in the hands of his sons, and shall wave them as a wave offering before the Lord.**
>
> **And you shall take them from their hands, and offer them up in smoke on the altar on the burnt offering for a soothing aroma before the Lord; it is an offering by fire to the Lord.**
>
> **Then you shall take the breast of Aaron's ram of ordination, and wave it as a wave offering before the Lord; and it shall be your portion.**

SACRIFICES, OFFERINGS & RITUALS

And you shall consecrate the breast of the wave offering and the thigh of the heave offering which was waved and which was offered from the ram of ordination, from the one which was for Aaron and from the one which was for his sons.

And it shall be for Aaron and his sons as their portion forever from the sons of Israel, for it is a heave offering; and it shall be a heave offering from the sons of Israel from the sacrifices of their peace offerings, even their heave offering to the Lord.

Exodus 29:19-28 (NASB)

And you shall take the ram of ordination and boil its flesh in a holy place

And Aaron and his sons shall eat the flesh of the ram, and the bread that is in the basket, at the doorway of the tent of meeting.

Thus they shall eat those things by which atonement was made at their ordination and consecration; but a layman shall not eat them, because they are holy.

And if any of the flesh of ordination or any of the bread remains until morning, then you shall burn the remainder with fire; it shall not be eaten, because it is holy.

Exodus 29:31-34 (NASB)

And he brought the other ram, the ram of consecration: and Aaron and his sons laid their hands upon the head of the ram.

And he slew it; and Moses took of the blood of it, and put it upon the tip of Aaron's right ear, and upon the thumb of his right hand, and upon the great toe of his right foot.

And he brought Aaron's sons, and Moses put of the blood upon the tip of their right ear, and upon the thumbs of their right hands, and upon the great toes of their right feet: and Moses sprinkled the blood upon the altar round about.

And he took the fat, and the rump, and all the fat that was upon the inwards, and the caul above the liver, and the two kidneys, and their fat, and the right shoulder:

> And out of the basket of unleavened bread, that was before the LORD, he took one unleavened cake, and a cake of oiled bread, and one wafer, and put them on the fat, and upon the right shoulder:
>
> And he put all upon Aaron's hands, and upon his sons' hands, and waved them for a wave offering before the LORD.
>
> And Moses took them from off their hands, and burnt them on the altar upon the burnt offering: they were consecrations for a sweet savour: it is an offering made by fire unto the LORD.
>
> And Moses took the breast, and waved it for a wave offering before the LORD: for of the ram of consecration it was Moses' part; as the LORD commanded Moses.
>
> Leviticus 8:22-29

SIN OFFERING. The term "sin offering" is somewhat misleading. The purpose of this sacrifice (Leviticus 4-5:13) was not to atone for any kind of sin, as the name seems to imply. Crimes against other people were dealt with by appropriate punishments that did not involve sacrifice, while deliberate crimes against God (done "with a high hand") could not be sacrificially atoned for at all.

> But the soul that doeth ought presumptuously, whether he be born in the land, or a stranger, the same reproacheth the LORD; and that soul shall be cut off from among his people.
>
> Because he hath despised the word of the LORD, and hath broken his commandment, that soul shall utterly be cut off; his iniquity shall be upon him.
>
> Numbers 15:30-31

Rather, the sin offering was used to cleanse the sanctuary of impurity. For this reason, it was regularly offered at festivals (Numbers 28:15, 22, 30; 29:5, 11, 16, 19). As a private offering, the sin offering (or more properly, the purification offering) was brought when a person had unwittingly violated a prohibition (Leviticus 4:2) or for rites of cleansing (Lev. 12:6; 14:19, 22; 15:15, 30; 16:3, 5; Num. 6:14, 16), or when one had forgotten to cleanse oneself (Lev. 5:2-3), or failed to fulfill a vow (Lev. 5:4), or had not responded to a public adjuration (Lev. 5:1). When both the sin offering and the burnt offering were to be offered, the sin offering always came first; the altar had to be cleansed before other sacrifices could be offered on it (cf. Lev. 9:7-21; 14:19).

The animals used for the private sin offering varied with the status of the offender. The high priest or community as a whole offered a bull; a ruler offered a male goat, while a lay person brought a female goat or a ewe. The ritual also varied: when the community (or the high priest who represented it) had transgressed, the sanctuary itself was defiled; it was cleansed by sprinkling some of the bull's blood in front of the sanctuary veil and smearing it on the horns of the incense altar (Lev. 4:5-7, 16-18). The bull's meat could not be eaten, so it was burned outside the camp (Lev. 4:12, 21).

In the case of an individual, whether ruler or commoner, only the outer altar was defiled. It was cleansed by smearing the blood of the goat or ewe on the altar's horns, and the priest received the meat of the animal. In certain cases there was a provision for a less costly sin offering if the person were poor (Lev. 5:7-13; 12:8; 14:21-22).

The *GUILT OFFERING* (Lev. 5:14-6:7) was brought when one had desecrated some holy thing (Lev. 5:14) or perjured oneself (Lev. 6:2-5). Its purpose was the reparation of damages. The sacrifice consisted of a ram, offered in a manner similar to the peace offering (Lev. 7:2-7), but with the necessary addition of the offerer's confession of guilt, and the repayment of damages, plus a twenty percent fine. The priest who offered it received the meat (Lev. 7:7). Uniquely, this sacrifice could even be paid for in money (Lev. 5:18; cf. II Kings 12:16). It was always a private sacrifice.

In two special cases, that of the healed leper being cleansed and that of a Nazarite whose vow was desecrated by accidental contact with a corpse (which made one impure), the guilt offering was a male lamb (Lev. 14:12, 21; Num. 6:9, 12). Furthermore, in the leper's case, the blood of the guilt offering was also applied to the person's extremities as part of the cleansing ritual (Lev. 14:12-14, 25).

The CEREAL OFFERING (Lev. 2) was a vegetable counterpart to the burnt offerings. It could be raw, in which case frankincense was added, or cooked in various ways (baked, boiled, fried), but it could not be leavened or sweetened (Lev. 2:11). Oil was present whether the offering was cooked or raw. The flour used was usually wheat (semolina), but barley flour or parched grain could also be offered (Lev. 2:14). When the cereal offering was a poor person's substitute for the animal sin offering, the flour was offered dry, without oil and incense (Lev. 5:11; cf. also Num. 5:15). Only a handful of the cereal offering (together with all the incense, if present) was burned on the altar; the remainder went to the priest (Lev. 2:2-3; 6:14-16).

The sole exception was the priest's cereal offering; it was entirely burned since a priest could not profit from his own offering (Lev. 6:23).

According to Numbers 15, the burnt offering and the peace offering were normally accompanied by cereal offerings (mixed with oil) and wine libations ("drink offerings"). The amount of grain and wine depended on the type of animal being offered: the larger the species, the more grain and wine.

Temple Ritual

The daily ritual was as follows: every morning, the ashes on the sacrificial altar were cleared off and the fire was stoked (Lev. 6:10-13), and the daily burnt offering, a yearling male lamb plus its accompanying cereal and drink offerings, were offered (Lev. 6:8-13; Exod. 29:38-42; Num. 28:3-8). The high priest, dressed in his priestly garments (Exod. 28:29, 30, 35, 38), entered the sanctuary, trimmed the oil lamps, and offered a specially formulated incense on the incense altar inside (Exod. 30:7-9, 34-36).

Outside, he would offer a special cereal offering composed of wheaten cakes cooked on a griddle (Lev. 6:19-23). In the evening, a second lamb was offered like the morning one, and the high priest again entered the sanctuary to trim the oil lamps (Lev. 24:1-4; cf. I Sam. 3:3) and burn incense. He would also offer the second half of the high-priestly cereal offering.

Such was the daily routine. Every Sabbath day two additional lambs were offered, like the daily ones (Num. 28:9-10). Also, the high priest would replace the twelve loaves of bread (the Bread of Presence), which were arranged in two rows on the table inside the sanctuary with frankincense on top (Lev. 24:5-9; cf. I Sam. 21:1-6). At the beginning of each month (the new moon) and at all the festivals, the priests blew trumpets (Num. 10:8, 10) and additional sacrifices were offered, both burnt offerings and a sin offering (which was always a male goat; see Num. 28-29). Festival days (or the beginning and end of week-long festivals) were days of rest like the Sabbath (Lev. 23:7-8, 21, 24, 27, 35, 36).

On the Day of Atonement the people rested and fasted and the high priest, wearing special garments for the occasion, performed the Day of Atonement ritual (Lev. 16) which cleansed the sanctuary of all impurity. It consisted of two sin offerings— one for the high priest and one for the people— whose blood was brought not only into the sanctuary but into the inner shrine itself, the Holy of Holies where the Ark of God was kept.

The high priest entered the Holy of Holies only after placing a pan of burning incense inside, to make a screen of smoke between him and the Ark (Lev. 16:13). After cleansing the sanctuary, the priest laid his hands on a living goat and confessed the people's sins, thereby transferring those sins to the goat, which was then sent away into the wilderness.

Donations

In addition to these public and private sacrifices, offered at regular seasons or at will, the people donated a tenth portion of their produce to the sanctuary. This tithe was given to the Levites in exchange for their work in guarding and transporting the tabernacle.

And, behold, I have given the children of Levi all the tenth in Israel for an inheritance, for their service which they serve, even the service of the tabernacle of the congregation.

Neither must the children of Israel henceforth come nigh the tabernacle of the congregation, lest they bear sin, and die.

But the Levites shall do the service of the tabernacle of the congregation, and they shall bear their iniquity: it shall be a statute for ever throughout your generations, that among the children of Israel they have no inheritance.

But the tithes of the children of Israel, which they offer as an heave offering unto the LORD, I have given to the Levites to inherit: therefore I have said unto them, Among the children of Israel they shall have no inheritance.

Numbers 18:21-24

And to the sons of Levi, behold, I have given all the tithe in Israel for an inheritance, in return for their service which they perform, the service of the tent of meeting.

And the sons of Israel shall not come near the tent of meeting again, lest they bear sin and die.

Only the Levites shall perform the service of the tent of meeting, and they shall bear their iniquity; it shall be a perpetual statute throughout your generations, and among the sons of Israel they shall have no inheritance.

For the tithe of the sons of Israel, which they offer as an offering to the Lord, I have given to the Levites for an inheritance; therefore I have said concerning them, They shall have no inheritance among the sons of Israel.

Numbers 18:21-24 (NASB)

The Levites themselves gave a tithe of their tithe to the priests.

Thus speak unto the Levites, and say unto them, When ye take of the children of Israel the tithes which I have given you from them for your inheritance, then ye shall offer up an heave offering of it for the LORD, even a tenth part of the tithe.

Numbers 18:26

Moreover, you shall speak to the Levites and say to them, When you take from the sons of Israel the tithe which I have given you from them for your inheritance, then you shall present an offering from it to the Lord, a tithe of the tithe.

Numbers 18:26 (NASB)

SACRIFICES, OFFERINGS & RITUALS

Furthermore, the priests received the first fruits of all produce, including a sheaf of grain at the beginning of the harvest and two loaves of leavened bread at its end (Lev. 23:10-11, 17; cf. Num. 18:11), the firstborn of all livestock (Num. 18:12-13, 15-17), and the first part of the processed produce (flour, wine, oil; cf. Num. 15:17-21; 18:12).

People might also voluntarily donate items to the sanctuary, which would then belong to the priests. If persons or non-sacrificial animals were donated, only the monetary value was paid.

> **And the LORD spake unto Moses, saying,**
> **Speak unto the children of Israel, and say unto them, When a man shall make a singular vow, the persons shall be for the LORD by thy estimation.**
>
> **And thy estimation shall be of the male from twenty years old even unto sixty years old, even thy estimation shall be fifty shekels of silver, after the shekel of the sanctuary.**
>
> **And if it be a female, then thy estimation shall be thirty shekels.**
>
> **And if it be from five years old even unto twenty years old, then thy estimation shall be of the male twenty shekels, and for the female ten shekels.**
>
> **And if it be from a month old even unto five years old, then thy estimation shall be of the male five shekels of silver, and for the female thy estimation shall be three shekels of silver.**
>
> **And if it be from sixty years old and above; if it be a male, then thy estimation shall be fifteen shekels, and for the female ten shekels.**
>
> **But if he be poorer than thy estimation, then he shall present himself before the priest, and the priest shall value him; according to his ability that vowed shall the priest value him.**
>
> Leviticus 27:1-8

> **Again, the Lord spoke to Moses, saying**
>
> **Speak to the sons of Israel, and say to them, 'When a man makes a difficult vow, he shall be valued according to your valuation of persons belonging to the Lord.**

> If your valuation is of the male from twenty years even to sixty years old, then your valuation shall be fifty shekels of silver, after the shekel of the sanctuary
>
> Or if it is a female, then your valuation shall be thirty shekels.
>
> And if it be from five years even to twenty years old then your valuation for the male shall be twenty shekels, and for the female ten shekels.
>
> But if they are from a month even up to five years old, then your valuation shall be five shekels of silver for the male, and for the female your valuation shall be three shekels of silver.
>
> And if they are from sixty years old and upward, if it is a male, then your valuation shall be fifteen shekels, and for the female ten shekels.
>
> But if he is poorer than your valuation, then he shall be placed before the priest, and the priest shall value him; according to the means of the one who vowed, the priest shall value him.
>
> **Leviticus 27:1-8 (NASB)**

Land, tithes of vegetable produce, and non-sacrificial animals could also be redeemed from the sanctuary by the donor, by paying the value plus a twenty percent penalty (Lev. 27:13, 19, 31). An extreme form of dedication was "devotion," which, when applied to cities, involved complete destruction (Num. 21:2-3; cf. Josh. 6:17-21). Anything so devoted could not be redeemed; persons who were devoted had to be killed (Lev. 27:28-29).

A different kind of dedication of a person was the Nazarite vow (Num. 6). People who made this vow could not drink any alcoholic beverage or consume any product of the grapevine, nor could they cut their hair or shave. In fact, the hair was actually consecrated to God (Num. 6:5, 9, 18). The Nazarites were holy and hence were not supposed to become unclean. The vow was of limited duration and at the end of the term a special ceremony was performed to return the Nazarite to ordinary, common status (Num. 6:13-20).

SACRIFICES, OFFERINGS & RITUALS

Ritual Purity

Persons participating in worship had to be ritually clean. Contact with a corpse (Num. 19) or animal carcasses (Lev. 11:8, 24-25, 31, 39), sexual emissions (Lev. 15), giving birth to a child (Lev. 12), and leprosy (Lev. 13) all caused a person to become unclean in various degrees. An unclean person could not eat sacrificial meat (Lev. 7:20), enter the sanctuary, or even handle tithes or other items belonging to God (Lev. 12:4). Cleansing was effected by bathing and washing one's clothes. Certain more severe states of impurity required additional rites of cleansing and might take several days to complete. Although one was excluded from worship, being unclean was not a crime. Failure to cleanse oneself after the period of impurity had passed, however, was sinful and necessitated bringing a sin offering (Lev. 5:2-3), since (prolonged) impurity defiled the sanctuary (cf. Lev. 16:19; Num. 19:20).

To be eligible to officiate in the sanctuary, priests were required not only to be clean but unblemished (Lev. 21:17-23). Furthermore, they could not officiate while drunk (Lev. 10:9) or mourning (Lev. 10:6). They had to be properly dressed (Exod. 28:40-43); and before officiating at either the altar or inside the sanctuary they were to wash their hands and feet (Exod. 30:18-21; priests did not wear shoes: cf. Exod. 3:5; Josh. 5:15).

Other Versions of Ritual Procedures

The book of Deuteronomy presents a slightly modified (though much less detailed) version of the system described by the Priestly texts. The principal difference lies in Deuteronomy's insistence on a single sanctuary for the entire land of Israel to which all sacrifices were to be brought (cf. Deut. 12:5-14). As a result, Deuteronomy permitted profane slaughter of animals for meat (Deut. 12:15 Lev. 17:2-4), since for many Israelites the distance to the sanctuary was too great (Deut. 12:20-21). There were also other, relatively minor differences in detail in Deuteronomy, regarding the Passover (Deut. 16:2 Exod. 12:5; Deut. 16:7 Exod. 12:9), tithes (Deut. 14:22-29 Num. 18), and the priests' share of sacrifices (Deut. 18:2 Lev. 7:31-32).

Worship in Ezekiel's visionary temple (Ezek. 40-48) also differs somewhat from the Priestly system. For instance, Ezekiel calls for a purification of the temple on the first and seventh days of the first month, presumably in preparation for the Passover (Ezek. 45:18-20; cf. 21). He also mentions only a single daily burnt offering sacrificed each morning (Ezek. 46:13-15). Ezekiel's system was never actually put into effect, but it may reflect the thinking of certain priests of his time, since Ezekiel himself was a priest (Ezek. 1:3).

Patriarchal Period

Actual practice also deviated somewhat from the Priestly system outlined above. The worship practiced by the patriarchs knows nothing of all this. Their worship was simple and informal; they had no priests or temples. Rather, the patriarchs themselves offered burnt offerings at temporary altars they built themselves in the open (cf. Gen. 8:20; 12:7-8; 13:18; 22:13; 26:25). Jacob also worshipped by pouring a drink offering on a pillar he set up and by anointing it with oil (Gen. 28:18; 35:14). In later periods this would probably have been considered idolatrous (Exod. 23:24; Deut. 7:5; I Kings 14:22-23).

The Period of the Judges

During the time of the judges this type of worship continued to be practiced, but priests and temples were also known. Levites were considered the proper people to act as priests (Judg. 17:13), but individual Israelites continued to offer their own sacrifices on simple outdoor altars (Judg. 6:24-27; 13:19). There was a temple at Shiloh during this period, where the Ark of the Lord was kept until it was captured by the Philistines. The account in I Samuel 1-3 provides a glimpse of temple worship at this time: families such as Samuel's might go there for a yearly feast, where they would offer sacrifice like a peace offering and perhaps pray, as Hannah did. The priests there took a portion of the meat, whatever "the fork brought up" (I Sam. 2:13-14). As in Leviticus the animal's suet belonged to God. It was to be offered first, after which the priest could take his share. Eli's sons were condemned for disregarding this rule and thereby slighting God (I Sam. 2:15-17).

First and Second Temple Times

Even after Solomon built the Temple in Jerusalem and installed the Ark there, the people continued to offer sacrifices at local outdoor altars ("high places"). After Solomon's death (924 B.C.), Jeroboam, king of Israel, built two shrines of his own at Bethel and Dan, for fear that the people, by worshipping in Jerusalem, would defect to the Davidic kings there (I Kings 12:26-29). Jeroboam also appointed non-Levites as priests (I Kings 12:31) and moved the Feast of Booths to the eighth month (I Kings 12:32-33). The writers of Kings and Chronicles condemned both Jeroboam's shrines and the "high places" as idolatrous (I Kings 14:23; 15:14; II Kings 12:3; 14:4; 15:4). The "high places" were too often associated with the pillars and other pagan practices (I Kings 14:23-24; II Kings 15:3-4), while Jeroboam's shrines were condemned for the calf images he erected at them (I Kings 12:31; 14:9). Under Josiah these "high places" were finally eradicated, and worship was centralized at the Jerusalem Temple (II Kings 23:5-9), as prescribed in Deuteronomy. However, the people continued to offer cereal offerings and incense privately, since there was no blood involved (cf. Jer. 41:4-5, where these offerings are brought to a ruined temple). This practice persisted even in Second Temple times.

An important element of Israelite worship hardly mentioned at all in the Pentateuch is that of prayer and song. Presumably the precise form of prayers or songs was not crucial to orthodox worship; the only recorded prayers are the priestly benediction (Num. 6:24-26) and prayers accompanying the offering of first fruits (Deut. 26:3-11) and tithes (Deut. 26:13-15). The Chronicler records the establishment of Levitical singers in the Temple (I Chron. 16:4-6), and many of the Psalms were probably composed for use in Temple worship. Individuals would naturally resort to the Temple to pray (cf. I Sam. 1:9-18; I Kings 8:22; 27-30), but prayer was a private matter and could be done anywhere. Fasting, too, was a private matter (e.g., II Sam. 12:16, 21-23), except on the Day of Atonement or when a special day of fasting was proclaimed (Joel 1:14; Ezra 8:21; II Chron. 20:3).

It is difficult to ascertain to what extent the rituals performed in Solomon's Temple corresponded to the instructions of the Pentateuch. For instance, there may have been only one daily burnt offering (cf. Ezek. 46:13-15) offered every morning, rather than two, with only a cereal offering presented in the evening (II Kings 16:15; cf. Ezra 9:5; Ps. 141:2; Dan. 9:21; where the "evening sacrifice" is literally the evening cereal offering). In Second Temple times, the Pentateuchal instructions were followed in detail in Temple worship. In addition, new festivals were added, two of which are mentioned in the Bible: Purim (Esther 9:20-22) and the Feast of Dedication (Hanukkah; cf. John 10:22-23).

A completely new institution of worship was added in the Second Temple period: the synagogue. Its origins are unknown but it probably began among the exiles, who were otherwise unable to worship, since they were too far from the Temple. The people gathered at the synagogue on the Sabbath to pray and read the Bible, and the Scripture reading was interpreted and expounded in a short sermon (cf. Luke 4:16-29).

Early Christian Worship

In the Old Testament "worship" still means primarily "bow down" but the word also translates Greek terms signifying service or piety. However, the external form of worship differs radically from that of the early Christians. Since the death of Christ constituted the perfect sacrifice, no more sacrifices were needed (Heb. 9:11-12, 24-26). Indeed, the entire institution of temple, priesthood, sacrifice, and cleansing ritual became obsolete. Rather, the Church itself, that is, all the believers, was at once temple and priesthood, inhabited by the Holy Spirit (I Cor. 6:19; Eph. 2:21-22; I Pet. 2:9).

As a result, Christian worship was internal rather than external. Only three rituals are known from the Old Testament: baptism, communion, and the laying on of hands. However, for none of these do we have any explicit instructions describing how they are to be performed. Baptism initiated a person into the church. It consisted simply of immersion in water and was probably accompanied by a reference to Jesus, in whose Name the person was baptized. The laying on of hands was associated with receiving spiritual gifts (Acts 8:17) or a special commission (Acts 13:2-3). Only communion was celebrated on a regular basis to commemorate Jesus' death and as a joyous anticipation of the future kingdom feast (cf. Mark 14:25; I Cor. 11:26). It consisted of a simple meal of bread and wine over which a blessing was spoken (I Cor. 10:16).

The first day of the week was a favorite day for Christian assembly (Acts 20:7; cf. I Cor. 16:2), though early Christians might also have met daily (Acts 2:46). At these meetings, there would be teaching, exhortation, singing, praying, prophesying, reading letters and the "breaking of bread" (probably communion; Acts 2:42, 46; 15:30; I Cor. 14:26; Col. 4:16). Above all, Christian worship was characterized by great joy and thanksgiving (cf. I Thess. 5:16-18).

CHAPTER IV

LET US WORSHIP HIM

> But the hour cometh, and now is, when the true worshippers shall worship the Father in spirit and in truth: for the Father seeketh such to worship him.
>
> **John 4:23**

This is one of the most often used Scriptures when the subject of worship is discussed. I believe that we, the Church, have yet to fulfill this Scripture. It is almost inconceivable that God is seeking for individuals that He deems as worshippers. You mean that the infinite, Almighty God, who is in need of nothing, is looking for vessels of worship? Yes! The heart cry of the Father will never be fulfilled until true worshippers are raised up in the Body of Christ.

Since it appears that it is so close to the end of the Church Age, I believe that God is now preparing His bride to fulfill John 4:23. This explains the reason why we are becoming so aware of the need of worship in our own lives. There seems to be such a real sense of attention given to this subject. People all over the world are beginning to sense an urgency, a hunger about training in the mechanics of worship.

We must realize that in order for us to worship Him, we must be willing to change. Warning! Change is very difficult, but change is good and inevitable! It remains a challenge to change our lives to something more glorious, to a life that God intended for us to have, a life that flows close to Him, a life that runs parallel with His ways and not contradictory. God wants us to draw closer to Him, become more intimate with Him. This He wants so that He can draw near to us and thus fulfill that desire for intimate fellowship that He has always longed for. In fact, this same fellowship that He desires is the fellowship He had in mind when He created you and me.

Worship is the outpouring or outflowing of the entire being: spirit, soul and body, under a sense of divine favor in the presence of Almighty

God. Worship is all that we are, reacting to all that He is. Worship is the overflow of our understanding of God as He has revealed Himself in His Word and as He has demonstrated His Word in our lives. To worship is to quicken the consciousness by the holiness of God, to feed the mind with the very truth of God, to purge the imagination by the beauty of God, to open the heart to the love of God and to devote the will to the purpose of God.

The Etymology of "Worship"

A thorough word study of worship unfolds some exciting truths about genuine worship. Several words have been translated "worship" in both the Old and New Testaments, thus the Hebrew and Greek. We can find the following in the King James Version of the Bible:

HEBREW WORD STUDY

SHACHAH

>And Abraham said unto his young men, Abide ye here with the ass; and I and the lad will go yonder and worship (Shachah) and come again to you.
>
>**Genesis 22:5**

>For thou shalt worship (Shachah) no other God: for the LORD, whose name is Jealous, is a jealous God:
>
>**Exodus 34:14**

>And he said, Nay; but as captain of the host of the LORD am I now come. And Joshua fell on his face to the earth, and did worship (Shachah) and said unto him, What saith my lord unto his servant?
>
>**Joshua 5:14**

>O come, let us worship (Shachah) and bow down: let us kneel before the LORD our maker.
>
>**Psalm 95:6**

Used 55 times, SHACHAH is by far the most common word translated "worship" and means "to bow down, prostrate, to fall on knees with forehead touching the ground, to fall flat, to reverence."

The picture we imagine is of one who would pay homage to a great king by bowing down before him, but of course our King is God Almighty.

It is believed that true worship will always include the realization of our existence to the place where every word of adoration is the privilege of those whose very life is held in the hands of Almighty God. The privilege in life is not to live but to worship, for in worship we find life at its fullest.

To SHACHAH is the only response one can have in the presence of God. So much more has been written in regard to praise than to worship principally because of the simplicity of worship. It requires no faith and little action, only reverence and prostration before Almighty God. It is the place where we simply fall at God's feet in wonder, awe and adoration.

And when I saw him, I fell at his feet as dead. And he laid his right hand upon me, saying unto me, Fear not; I am the first and the last:

Revelation 1:17

Revelation 1:17 describes the reaction that would be most normal when God has presented Himself in our midst. Worship is our response to God's presence and nothing means more to a true worshipper than being in the presence of the Lord (Philippians 2:9-11).

God's original intention for His people was that they be a kingdom of priests and they would know God as Moses knew Him.

> And ye shall be unto me a kingdom of priests, and an holy nation. These are the words which thou shalt speak unto the children of Israel.
>
> Exodus 19:6

Can you imagine that? God wants us to know Him face to face as Moses did. Worshippers who know Him face to face is what the last generation will be. If we don't reach that place, we will be the New Testament believers who have a better covenant, but an inferior fellowship with God. The Old Testament worshippers knew Him as God only, yet we have been told to love Him as Father. There is no comparison in the Old Testament contact with God and New Testament contact with the Father. We must see this reality and flow into it. Nothing less will satisfy the Father's heart.

CEGID

Used 8 times, the word corresponds to the Hebrew word CAGAD. It is translated much less frequently as worship than SHACHAH and means to "prostrate oneself in homage, to fall down." It is almost entirely used in connection with idol worship of the golden image of Nebuchadnezzar in the Book of Daniel. The conversation is between king Nebuchadnezzar and the three Hebrew boys (Shadrach, Meshach and Abednego) when this word CAGAD is used. The same word is interpreted "worshipped" and "worshippeth" but is not used outside of the Book of Daniel.

ATSAB

This word is used only once and that is in connection with idols. From this brief study we summarize by saying that only one word really interests us as worshipping believers and that is SHACHAH. We should therefore study the references to this word and be aware of its meaning when we worship the Most High God.

GREEK WORD STUDY

PROSKUNEO

Again, we find a Greek word translated as worship which is used much more frequently than any of the others. PROSKUNEO means "fawn or crouch, to prostrate oneself in homage, to do reverence or to adore." The word is taken from a word meaning to kiss, like a dog licking his master's hand. The strongest picture we can imagine between a man and his dog is this one. It gives an indication of the love that there can be between a man and his dog. How much more then is there love between our Heavenly Father and His children. We are not dogs to Master, we are His blood-bought children, and when we PROSKUNEO, we are in our Daddy's lap and He is tenderly holding us and loving us.

This is a true picture of worship: it is not some distant thing, but an intimate thing between an intimately loving Heavenly Father and His loving child.

Jesus used the word PROSKUNEO in John 4 in his discussion with the woman at the well in Samaria. The devil used this word in Luke 4:7-8 when he asked Jesus to worship him and it is this worship that he craves. When man worships idols the devil would like to believe that he is receiving PROSKUNEO from them but he never will since PROSKUNEO can only be performed in mutual love.

It is also interesting to note that the word PROSKUNEO is used exclusively in the book of Revelation where worship or worshipped is mentioned.

LATREUO

This word is translated as worship 3 times. It means "to minister to God, to render religious homage, serve, do the service, worship."

THE MECHANICS OF TRUE WORSHIP

> But Peter, standing up with the eleven, lifted up his voice, and said unto them, Ye men of Judaea, and all ye that dwell at Jerusalem, be this known unto you, and hearken to my words:
>
> Acts 2:14

Paul's reply to the governor is that he worships (Latreuo) just as his ancestors did. Paul was talking here about his life of service to God. This is what worship is all about: it's a life of service, a continuous life attitude. In verse 11, Paul states that he went up to Jerusalem to PROSKUNEO and then refers to his worship as LATREUO in verse 14. What I believe he was saying was that PROSKUNEO is a type of life service of LATREUO that he lived.

The word LATREUO has the connotation of a service as a bond-slave, completely sold out to his lord and his master. We could say "a willing slave to worship."

SEBOMAI

The word means "to revere, adore," stressing the feeling of awe or devotion. It is used as follows in the King James Version:

WORSHIP	Matthew 15:9
	Mark 7:7
	Acts 18:13
WORSHIPPED	Acts 16:14
	Acts 18:7
WORSHIPPETH	Acts 19:27
	Acts 18:13

OTHER LESS COMMON WORDS

DOXA

DOXA is most often interpreted "glory" but is interpreted once as worship in Luke 14:10:

But when thou art bidden, go and sit down in the lowest room; that when he that bade thee cometh, he may say unto thee, Friend, go up higher: then shalt thou have worship in the presence of them that sit at meat with thee.

Luke 14:10

EUSEBEO

To act pious toward God or respectfully, used in:

For as I passed by, and beheld their devotions, I found an altar with this inscription, TO THE UNKNOWN GOD. Whom therefore ye ignorantly worship, him declare I unto you.

Acts 17:23

ENOPION

Before or in the presence of, used in Luke 4:7:

If thou therefore wilt worship me, all shall be thine.

ETHELOTHRESKIA

Voluntarily will to worship, used in

Which things have indeed a shew of wisdom in will worship, and humility, and neglecting the body; not in any honour to the satisfying of the flesh.

Colossians 2:23

CHAPTER V

THE DIFFERENCE BETWEEN PRAISE AND WORSHIP

Praise is an operation of faith which will create conditions for God to inhabit our presence. We see praise being offered to God in varying circumstances of need, testing, warfare, celebrations, etc. and in many instances praise works for us against the enemy and will always affect him. It seems that the devil is still in the fight to some extent in the realm of praise, but in worship we never consider him.

In worship we are so entrenched and so close to God that the devil does not come close to us. Praise fortifies our lives against the work of the enemy and neutralizes his presence and power to work against us. Worship however has brought us to a realm where the devil has been dismissed already and we are standing in the presence of God.

I am not suggesting that a worshipper won't be tempted, I am saying that in worship the worshipper is not concerned or preoccupied with the devil but only with our Heavenly Father and the Lord Jesus Christ. Worship is the expression of our response to His presence, after His presence has come. There is no work involved in worship. It rests in the Holy Spirit who takes us in the Holy of Holies.

Praise often involves sacrifice, but worship doesn't involve sacrifice and nowhere in the Bible will we find a sacrifice of worship. When we enter into worship our sacrifice, as it were, has been accepted and received and we are behind the veil. We do not give God the sacrifice of love. Either we love Him or we do not worship Him at all. Worship is never something we do because we have to, but because we deeply desire to.

While obedience to God's Word would be the catalyst for praise, a love for God is the catalyst for worship. Without any hint of disrespect we could liken praise to dating and worship to marriage. Many of us have had dates that we didn't make any real commitment to, but only a fool would marry someone that he/she does not love. God has many children who date Him and He loves them, but He is looking for those He can marry. I hope you understand my meaning when I use this kind of terminology.

We cannot be true worshippers until we have first had an experience in praise. When two people are in love they begin to talk about each other, extolling each other's virtues and their speech indicates that a love relationship is developing. The same is true of our relationship with Jesus. As we learn to know Him, we extol His virtues and we begin to audibly praise His name. As our relationship with Jesus deepens, our worship increases and as we get to know Him in a more intimate way we pour our hearts out to Him in worship.

Worship is a thing of the heart and it will always be a motivator to worship. Even if we don't go through all the so-called steps to worship and don't do all the physical expressions, we can still be in worship because of the right heart attitude. God always looks at the heart and I praise Him for that because my head and my body disappoint Him at times. You and I can sometimes say wrong things but if our hearts are pure before Him we get by.

If we keep these hearts of ours pure before God continually, everything else will get into line. It's really simple: If you love God (heart) you won't allow that love relationship to be strained in any way through your mind or body. Let the heart rule in worship!

Another area of concern is the liberal and erroneous distinction the Body of Christ makes, generally speaking, with regard to fast choruses being praise and slow ones being worship. Speed has nothing to do with the category. The important distinction between praise and worship is not the particular speed or expression that is manifested in a service, but the fact that while praise is operated as an act of faith creating the presence of God, worship is the expression of our response to His presence.

We could very well respond to His presence in a fast moving chorus or quite equally in a ballad-type song. The important point here is a recognition of faith principal. While we are still operating in faith, we are in the realm of praise until we reach **Tehillah (High Praise).**

When our faith is no longer operational, we are in the area of worship. Let me clarify this point. It doesn't mean that if we don't have faith, we cannot enter into worship because it is basically a condition of the heart that God is looking at. But it should be evident that a right heart relationship and fellowship with God will be one of faith, for without faith it is impossible to please God.

WORSHIP IS A DIVINE CYCLE OF GIVING!

Worship completes a divine cycle of giving when we consider that the spiritual life that flows from God to us returns to Him in worship from us, and thus the divine cycle is complete.

1. It all started with God who gave His all to man through Jesus.

2. Jesus gave His all to us (His life).

3. Man gives his all (in worship) back to God by the help of the Holy Spirit.

4. God gives more back to man through Jesus.

When we minister to the Lord we enter into a divine cycle of giving to Him and receiving from Him. It's the receiving of spiritual life from Him that can enable us to do anything. If we are not receiving in our giving we are deceived and are in a useless programme of good works that will destroy us. God doesn't need born again strangers to work for Him. Many who toil in the cloth are strangers to Him.

There's a difference between working in a big company and never meeting the Managing Director again after your initial interview, or being in a working situation where the Managing Director and you are partners, co-laborers working together.

God wants us to be in His flow. He wants us to be in a situation where He can flow His life through ours and we become a duplicate of His life, instead of trying to duplicate His work. This is a problem with many of us— we are trying to duplicate the works of Jesus instead of simply allowing His life to flow through us. I am convinced that the end-time worshipper will concentrate on the life of God in Him, rather that the works of God through Him.

The end-time worshipper will indeed have the life and nature of God and be changed into the same image from glory to glory, but those who refuse this opportunity to worship will not reflect His glory and likeness. Whenever we go into the presence of the Lord or whenever we gather together, God will give us a revelation of His nature, character and person. These are automatically flowing to us when we spend time with Him, so that we automatically become like Him.

He has left the choice with us. If we want to be men and women who do great works for God, that's great and God will bless us and the world will praise us, but there is something greater. There's the place where we can have the nature of God and glorify Him in every action, gesture, word and deed. It's that place of worship. It's that place of rest and not work, never trying to be like God but just simply worshipping Him.

WORSHIP IS A FLOW IN THE HOLY SPIRIT

The spiritual life that flows from God to us returns to Him in worship from us. In John 4, Jesus used the term "living water" to define the spiritual life that He has gives to us. Some may find it questionable as to whether Jesus is the Living Water or not, but I think that His is since He said He would have given it to the woman of Samaria if she had asked. He could not have been referring to the Holy Spirit since the Holy Spirit was not available at that time for anyone to receive.

THE DIFFERENCE BETWEEN PRAISE AND WORSHIP

Let's look at John 6:32-35...

Then Jesus said unto them, Verily, verily, I say unto you, Moses gave you not that bread from heaven; but my Father giveth you the true bread from heaven.

For the bread of God is he which cometh down from heaven, and giveth life unto the world.

Then said they unto him, Lord, evermore give us this bread.

And Jesus said unto them, I am the bread of life: he that cometh to me shall never hunger; and he that believeth on me shall never thirst.

Here we see that Jesus is the bread of life but notice in verse 35 how He states that those who believe in Him will never thirst. He is also now the Living Water. Let's also look at John 7:38-39...

He that believeth on me, as the scripture hath said, out of his belly shall flow rivers of living water.

(But this spake he of the Spirit, which they that believe on him should receive: for the Holy Ghost was not yet given; because that Jesus was not yet glorified.)

The Holy Spirit is God— let us never forget that— that He has come to reveal Jesus. John 15:26...

But when the Comforter is come, whom I will send unto you from the Father, even the Spirit of truth, which proceedeth from the Father, he shall testify of me

DEFINITION OF PRAISE

Praise has some characteristics that we must understand and practice, i.e., praise is always active and demonstrative, involving movement, action, sounds and songs that are both seen and heard. It can be demonstrated in so many ways such as shouting, singing, kneeling, dancing, clapping, playing musical instruments, boasting, leaping, etc.

It may be audible without being vocal, i.e., clapping is audible but not vocal, but can never be vocal without being audible. It may be visible without being audible or vocal, e.g., kneeling, dancing.

To enhance the definition we could say the following: *Praise is to commend the merits of, to glorify, extol the attributes of God in a way that could be either vocal, visible, audible, or a combination of these.*

As an introduction to the subject of praise it is necessary that we study the meaning of the words of praise that God has given us in the Bible. Take a deep breath and let's plunge into the Hebrew word study of praise.

PRAISE: A WORD STUDY IN HEBREW

God has given us seven Hebrew words for praise that are more commonly used in connection with praise. We must therefore study these words and be aware of applying their meaning in our praise as instructed by the Holy Spirit. God would not have given us seven different ways to respond to Him in praise if He didn't expect us to do them. I know that as you study these words and apply them in your own devotional times they will become a reality to you and a blessing to God.

1. **HALLAL (Strongs' definition) (haw-lal'):**

    a primitive root; to be clear (orig. of sound, but usually of color); to shine; hence, to make a show, to boast; and thus to be (clamorously) foolish; to rave; causatively, to celebrate; also to stultify:

THE DIFFERENCE BETWEEN PRAISE AND WORSHIP

2. **HALLAL (King James Version)**

to (make) boast (self), celebrate, commend, (deal, make), fool (-ish, -ly), glory, give [light], be (make, feign oneself) mad (against), give in marriage, [sing, be worthy of] praise, rage, renowned, shine.

3. **HALLAL (Brown-Driver-Briggs' definition)**

1) to shine; (a) (Qal) to shine (figurative of God's favor) (b) (Hiphil) to flash forth light (2) to praise, to boast, to be boastful (a) (Qal) (1) to be boastful (2) boastful ones, boasters (participle) (b) (Piel) (1) to praise (2) to boast, to make a boast (c) (Pual) to be praised, to be made praiseworthy, to be commended, to be worthy of praise (d) (Hithpael) to boast, to glory, to make one's boast (e) (Poel) to make a fool of, to make into a fool (f) (Hithpoel) to act madly, to act like a madman.

HALLAL is used 99 times on the Old Testament, more than any of the other major words translated "praise." Almost one-third of the occurrences of this word in the Psalms are common to praise. The word means "to laud, boast, celebrate, be clamorously foolish, clear of sound, shine." The action that one seems to have in HALLAL praise is best explained by the way one acts when they have fallen in love: kind of foolish. Don't say you can't remember! If you are married, you went through it. God expects us to be so in love with Him that we boast and rave to the extent that the world calls us foolish. No, we are not being foolish, we are just being normal. It's reasonable service to be foolishly in love with God. There is no love affair in the world's greatest script written that could compare with the one we have with Father God.

In HALLAL, there is complete abandonment of self, we can't see ourselves or even bother about what others see in us because we are concerned only with God. Dizzily in love with Him. It's a manifestation of being drunk in the spirit.

HALLAL is used in conjunction with the Name of God "JAH" to form the most commonly used word in the Bible for praise— HALLELUJAH. The word HALLELUJAH has no languages. The word simply means the spontaneous outcry of one who is excited about God.

HALLELUJAH is used 24 times in the Psalms and occurs between Psalms 104 and 150 as follows: Psalm 104:13; 105:45; 106:1, 48; 111:1; 112:1; 113:1, 9; 115:18; 116:19; 117:2; 135:1, 3, 21; 146:1, 10; 147:1, 20; 148:1, 14; 149:1, 9; 150:1, 6.

> ONE Psalm contains Hallelujah within it (135)
> TWO Psalms begin with Hallelujah (111, 112)
> FIVE Psalms end with Hallelujah (104, 105; 115-117)
> EIGHT Psalms begin and end with Hallelujah (106; 113; 135; 146-150)

Hallelujah seems to be the only response to God's greatness and power, His majesty and glory, and His eternal state.

There is a "U" between these words. It takes you to make praise spontaneous and continuous— it does not just happen!

Here are some key passages using HALLAL:

And he appointed certain of the Levites to minister before the ark of the LORD, and to record, and to thank and praise the LORD God of Israel:

I Chronicles 16:4

In God I will praise his word, in God I have put my trust; I will not fear what flesh can do unto me.

Psalm 56:4

In God will I praise his word: in the LORD will I praise his word.

Psalm 56:10

Blessed are they that dwell in thy house: they will be still praising thee. Selah.

Psalm 84:4

This shall be written for the generation to come: and the people which shall be created shall praise the LORD.

Psalm 102:18

From the rising of the sun unto the going down of the same the LORD'S name is to be praised.

Psalm 113:3

You can also study the following references:

II Samuel 22:4; II Samuel 22:50; I Chronicles 16:25,36; 23:5,30; 25:3; 29:13; II Chronicles 7:6, 8, 24; 20:19, 21; 29:30; 30:21; Ezra 3:11; Nehemiah 5:13; Psalms 9:11; 18:3; 22:23, 26; 35:18; 48:1; 63:5; 69:30, 34; 74:21; 102:18; 104:35; 105:45; 106:1, 48; 107:32; 109:30; 111:1; 112:1; 113:1, 9; 115:18; 116:19; 117:2; 119:175; 135:1, 3, 21; 145:2, 3; 146:1, 2, 10; 147:1, 12, 20; 148:1, 5, 7, 13, 14; 149:1, 3, 9; 150:1-6; Isaiah 62:8-9; Jeremiah 20:13; Joel 2:26.

4. **YADAH (Brown-Driver-Briggs' definition) (ya-dah')**

   to throw, to shoot, to cast (a) (Qal) to shoot (arrows) (b) (Piel) to cast, to cast down, to throw down (c) (Hiphil) (1) to give thanks, to laud, praise (2) to confess, to confess (the name of God) (d) (Hithpael) (1) to confess (sin) (2) to give thanks

5. **YADAH (Strong's definition) (yaw-daw')**

   a primitive root; used only as denominative; literally, to use (i.e. hold out) the hand; physically, to throw (a stone, an arrow) at or away; especially to revere or worship (with extended hands); intensively, to bemoan (by wringing the hands).

6. **YADAH (King James Version)**

cast (out), (make) confess (-ion), praise, shoot, (give) thank (-ful, -s, -sgiving).

This is the second most frequently occurring word translated "praise" in the Old Testament. The words means to worship with extended hands, to throw out the hands, to give thanks to God." It is often translated "thanks or thanksgiving" in the English translations. It is obvious from verses in the Old Testament that the lifting of hands was of some significance in praise. It seems to be most offensive to those who have never done it. Some references to this act of hand lifting:

Lift up your hands in the sanctuary, and bless the LORD.

Psalm 134:2

And Ezra blessed the LORD, the great God. And all the people answered, Amen, Amen, with lifting up their hands: and they bowed their heads, and worshipped the LORD with their faces to the ground.

Nehemiah 8:6

Thus will I bless thee while I live: I will lift up my hands in thy name.

Psalm 63:4

I will therefore that men pray every where, lifting up holy hands, without wrath and doubting.

I Timothy 2:8

This exercise is one of the most explosive and meaningful expressions of praise! God loves it, the flesh hates it, and the devil is devastated by it. Our hands give us away. As no other part of our bodies they are an extension of our personalities. When we feel embarrassed we don't know what to do with our hands. We use them in walking, working, communicating. We use them to express ourselves. An angry man clenches his fists, threatening to do damage with them.

A guilty man seeks to hide his hands. A worried person wrings his hands as if to rub some hope out in the open. A man in desperation tends to throw his hands up in resignation. A man uses his hands to welcome and entreat, inviting other hands to clasp his. An accusing person points a finger. The raising of hands is an international sign of surrender and in this expression of raised hands to the Lord in praise we are showing complete surrender to Him.

The word YADAH is used over 90 times in the Old Testament. YAD means "hand" and thus in the lengthened form is translated "to throw, to cast, or to shoot." It is translated "praise" 54 times in the King James Version, as "give thanks" 32 times, as "thanks" 5 times, and as "confess" 16 times.

Here are some key passages using YADAH:

And she conceived again, and bare a son: and she said, Now will I praise the LORD: therefore she called his name Judah; and left bearing.

Genesis 29:35

And when he had consulted with the people, he appointed singers unto the LORD, and that should praise the beauty of holiness, as they went out before the army, and to say, Praise the LORD; for his mercy endureth for ever.

2 Chronicles 20:21

To the chief Musician upon Muthlabben, A Psalm of David.
I will praise thee, O LORD, with my whole heart; I will shew forth all thy marvellous works.

Psalm 9:1

I will praise thee for ever, because thou hast done it: and I will wait on thy name; for it is good before thy saints.

Psalm 52:9

Oh that men would praise the LORD for his goodness, and for his wonderful works to the children of men!

> Psalm 107:8

Oh that men would praise the LORD for his goodness, and for his wonderful works to the children of men!

Oh that men would praise the LORD for his goodness, and for his wonderful works to the children of men!

Oh that men would praise the LORD for his goodness, and for his wonderful works to the children of men!

> Psalm 107:15, 21, 31

I will praise thee; for I am fearfully and wonderfully made: marvellous are thy works; and that my soul knoweth right well.

> Psalm 139:14

All thy works shall praise thee, O LORD; and thy saints shall bless thee.

> Psalm 145:10

7. **BARAK (Strong's definition) (baw-rak')**

   a primitive root; to kneel; by implication to bless God (as an act of adoration), and (vice-versa) man (as a benefit); also (by euphemism) to curse (God or the king, as treason):

8. **BARAK (King James Version definition)**

   abundantly, altogether, at all, blaspheme, bless, congratulate, curse, X greatly, indeed, kneel (down), praise, salute, still, thank

9. **BARAK (Brown-Driver-Briggs' definition)**

   (1) to bless, to kneel (a) (Qal) (1) to kneel (2) to bless (b) (Niphal) to be blessed, to bless oneself (c) (Piel) to bless (d) (Pual) to be blessed, to be adored (e) (Hiphil) to cause to kneel (f) (Hithpael) to bless

oneself (2) Theological Wordbook of the Old Testament: to praise, to salute, to curse.

This is a vital word connected with praise in the Old Testament. It's uniqueness is enhanced when we discover that it is translated "praise" only rarely in the King James Version. Over 200 times it is used to denote blessing or blessings from God, as well as between people. It denotes praise to God approximately 70 times. It means "to kneel, to bless, to salute" or in rare instances "to curse."

The cases where BARAK is translated "praise" in the King James Version are:

Praise ye the LORD for the avenging of Israel, when the people willingly offered themselves.

Judges 5:2

And he shall live, and to him shall be given of the gold of Sheba: prayer also shall be made for him continually; and daily shall he be praised.

Psalm 72:15

The occasion of the first reference is the song of Deborah and Barak (whose very name means "bless"). Their song began with these words "that the leaders led in Israel, that the people volunteered, Bless *(barak)* the Lord." The other reference in Psalm 72:15 is to Solomon as the psalmist says "And he shall live, and to him shall be given of the gold of Sheba: prayer also shall be made for him continually; and daily shall he be praised."

There are several key references worthy of special notice. When David was raising the monies and materials for the building of the Temple, and after he had given from his own personal treasures a vast amount of gold and silver, the record goes that " wherefore David blessed the Lord before all the congregation: and David said Blessed be thou Lord God of Israel our father, for ever and ever (1 Chron.29:10).

THE MECHANICS OF TRUE WORSHIP

Here are some key passages using BARAK:

And said, Naked came I out of my mother's womb, and naked shall I return thither: the LORD gave, and the LORD hath taken away; blessed be the name of the LORD.
Job 1:21

Sing unto the LORD, bless his name; shew forth his salvation from day to day.
Psalm 96:2

Bless the LORD, O my soul: and all that is within me, bless his holy name.

Bless the LORD, O my soul, and forget not all his benefits:

Bless the LORD, ye his angels, that excel in strength, that do his commandments, hearkening unto the voice of his word.

Bless ye the LORD, all ye his hosts; ye ministers of his, that do his pleasure.

Bless the LORD, all his works in all places of his dominion: bless the LORD, O my soul.
Psalm 103:1, 2, 20, 21, 22

Bless the LORD, O my soul. O LORD my God, thou art very great; thou art clothed with honour and majesty.
Psalm 104:1

Other uses of Barak in the Old Testament:

Genesis 9:26; 14:20; 24:27; Exodus 18:10; I Samuel 25:32, 39; II Sam.18:28; I Kings 1:48; 5:7; 8:15, 56; 10:9; I Chronicles 16:36; II Chronicles 2:12; 6; 4; 9:8; Ezra 7:27; Psalms 16:7; 18:46; 26:12; 28:6; 31:21; 34:1; 66:8, 26; 68:26, 32, 53; 72:18-19; 89:52; 100:4b; 103:1, 2, 20-22; 104:1, 35; 106:48; 115:18; 119:12; 124:6; 134:1,2; 135:19-21; 144:1; 145:1, 2, 10, 21.

We are often called on to give testimony of the Lord's blessings on us, and we should never be without a word regarding this. However, it must be remembered that even here it is more blessed to give than to receive (Acts 20:35).

THE DIFFERENCE BETWEEN PRAISE AND WORSHIP

> **I have shewed you all things, how that so labouring ye ought to support the weak, and to remember the words of the Lord Jesus, how he said, It is more blessed to give than to receive.**
>
> **Acts 20:35**

That I can receive a blessing from the Lord is a welcome prospect. That I can be and give a blessing to the Lord is even more thrilling. If David blessed the Lord, so can you and I.

10. **TEHILLAH (Strong's definition) tehillah (the-hil-law')**

    laudation; specifically (concretely) a hymn:

11. **TEHILLAH (King James Version)**

    praise

12. **TEHILLAH (Brown-Driver-Briggs' definition)**

    praise, a song or a hymn of praise (a) praise, adoration, thanksgiving (paid to God) (b) the act of general or public praise (c) a praise-song (as a Hebrew title) (d) praise (demanded by qualities or deeds or attributes of God) (e) renown, fame, glory (1) used of Damascus, God (2) an object of praise, a possessor of renown (figurative).

TEHILLAH is the fourth most frequently used word relating to praise in the Old Testament, occurring over 50 times. It is derived from Hallal and is generally accepted as meaning the singing of "hallals." The word means to sing or laud. It is perceived as involving music, especially singing. TEHILLAH is the praise that God inhabits. God is not always manifest in the singing of the saints, but He is in TEHILLAH.

> **But thou art holy, O thou that inhabitest the praises of Israel.**
>
> **Psalm 22:3**

THE MECHANICS OF TRUE WORSHIP

We will study this word in greater detail a little later. Here are some key passages using TEHILLAH:

But thou art holy, O thou that inhabitest the praises of Israel.

Psalm 22:3

Praise ye the LORD: for it is good to sing praises unto our God; for it is pleasant; and praise is comely.

The LORD doth build up Jerusalem: he gathereth together the outcasts of Israel.

Psalm 147:1-2

Who is like unto thee, O LORD, among the gods? Who is like thee, glorious in holiness, fearful in praises, doing wonders?

Exodus 15:11

He is thy praise, and he is thy God, that hath done for thee these great and terrible things, which thine eyes have seen.

Deuteronomy 10:21

And to make thee high above all nations which he hath made, in praise, and in name, and in honour; and that thou mayest be an holy people unto the LORD thy God, as he hath spoken.

Deuteronomy 26:19

And say ye, Save us, O God of our salvation, and gather us together, and deliver us from the heathen, that we may give thanks to thy holy name, and glory in thy praise.

I Chronicles 16:35

And when they began to sing and to praise, the LORD set ambushments against the children of Ammon, Moab, and mount Seir, which were come against Judah; and they were smitten.

II Chronicles 20:22

THE DIFFERENCE BETWEEN PRAISE AND WORSHIP

Then the Levites, Jeshua, and Kadmiel, Bani, Hashabniah, Sherebiah, Hodijah, Shebaniah, and Pethahiah, said, Stand up and bless the LORD your God for ever and ever: and blessed be thy glorious name, which is exalted above all blessing and praise.

Nehemiah 9:5

For in the days of David and Asaph of old there were chief of the singers, and songs of praise and thanksgiving unto God.

Nehemiah 12:46

To appoint unto them that mourn in Zion, to give unto them beauty for ashes, the oil of joy for mourning, the garment of praise for the spirit of heaviness; that they might be called trees of righteousness, the planting of the LORD, that he might be glorified.

Isaiah 61:3

Other uses of TEHILLAH in the Old Testament:

Psalms 9:14; 22:35; 33:1; 34:1; 35:28; 40:3; 48:10; 51:15; 65;1; 68:1, 2, 8; 71:6, 8,14; 78:4; 100:4; 102:21; 106:1, 12, 47; 109:1; 111:10; 119:171; 145:21; 147:1 148:14; 149:1; Isaiah 42:8, 10, 12; 43:21; 48:9; 60:6, 18; 61:11; 62:7; 63:7; Jeremiah 13:11; 17:14; 33:9; 49:25; Habakkuk 3:3; Zephaniah 3:19-20.

13. **ZAMAR (Strong's definition) (zaw-mar')**

a primitive root [perhaps identified with 2168 through the idea of striking with the fingers]; properly, to touch the strings or parts of a musical instrument, i.e. play upon it; to make music, accompanied by the voice; hence to celebrate in song and music:

14. **ZAMAR (King James Version)**

give praise, sing forth praises, psalms.

15. **ZAMAR (Brown-Driver-Briggs' definition)**

to sing, to sing praise, to make music; (Piel) (1) to make music, to sing (2) to play a musical instrument.

This word is used almost exclusively in poetry. Its occurrence outside of Psalms is rare. It means to "pluck the strings of an instrument, to sing praise." It is a musical word and is largely involved with joyous expressions of music. It is used approximately 40 times in expression of praise, of which only 4 are outside of Psalms. It is used in I Chronicles 16:9, one of the greatest chapters of praise in the entire Bible: "Sing to Him, sing psalms (*zamar*) unto Him, talk ye of all His wondrous works."

Other uses of ZAMAR in the Old Testament:

Judges 5:3; II Samuel 22:50; Psalms 7:17; 9:2, 11; 18:49; 21:13; 27;6; 30:4, 12; 33:23; 47:6, 7; 57:7, 9; 61:8; 66:2, 4; 71:22, 23; 75:9; 98:4, 5; 101:1; 104:33; 105:2; 108:1, 3; 135:3; 138:1; 144:9; 146:2; 147:7; 149:3; Isaiah 12:5.

16. **TOWDAH (Strong's definition) (to-daw')**

properly, an extension of the hand, i.e. (by implication) avowal, or (usually) adoration; specifically, a choir of worshippers.

17. **TOWDAH (King James Version)**

confession, (sacrifice of) praise, thanks (-giving, offering).

18. **TOWDAH (Brown-Driver-Briggs' definition)**

confession, praise, thanksgiving (a) give praise to God (b) thanksgiving in songs of liturgical worship, a hymn of praise (c) a thanksgiving choir or a procession or a line or a company (d) a thank-offering, a sacrifice of thanksgiving (e) confession

THE DIFFERENCE BETWEEN PRAISE AND WORSHIP

The word is used in conjunction with an offering and can be taken to mean "to extend the hands in a sacrifice of praise, thanksgiving." In at least one case it seems to involve that which is not yet visible. It is an act of faith beyond which God moves to bring deliverance. This is seen in Psalm 50:23:

> **Whoso offereth praise glorifieth me: and to him that ordereth his conversation aright will I shew the salvation of God.**

It may be at this point that the "sacrifice of praise" is most significant. Here in TOWDAH we have the type of praise that does not yet see victory, the solution or the answer. Common sense, human visibilities and logic are sacrificed along with the thanks offering of TOWDAH.

It is both interesting and significant that this is the word used in Leviticus in connection with the offering of thanksgiving. These references are to the fellowship offering.

> **And this is the law of the sacrifice of peace offerings, which he shall offer unto the LORD.**
>
> **If he offer it for a thanksgiving, then he shall offer with the sacrifice of thanksgiving unleavened cakes mingled with oil, and unleavened wafers anointed with oil, and cakes mingled with oil, of fine flour, fried.**
>
> **Besides the cakes, he shall offer for his offering leavened bread with the sacrifice of thanksgiving of his peace offerings.**
>
> **And the flesh of the sacrifice of his peace offerings for thanksgiving shall be eaten the same day that it is offered; he shall not leave any of it until the morning.**
>
> **Leviticus 7:11-13, 15**

Here are some key passages using TOWDAH:

> **When I remember these things, I pour out my soul in me: for I had gone with the multitude, I went with them to the house of God, with the voice of joy and praise, with a multitude that kept holyday.**
>
> **Psalm 42:4**

THE MECHANICS OF TRUE WORSHIP

Offer unto God thanksgiving; and pay thy vows unto the most High:

Psalm 50:14

Thy vows are upon me, O God: I will render praises unto thee.

Psalm 56:12

Let us come before his presence with thanksgiving, and make a joyful noise unto him with psalms.

Psalm 95:2

Some other uses of TOWDAH in the Old Testament:

Leviticus 22:29; II Chronicles 29;31; 33:16; Nehemiah 12:27, 31, 38, 40; Psalms.26;7; 69:30; 107:22; 116:17; Isaiah 51:3; Jeremiah 17:26; 33:11; Amos 4:5.

19. **SHABACH (Strong's definition) (shaw-bakh')**

a primitive root; properly, to address in a loud tone, i.e. (specifically) loud; figuratively, to pacify (as if by words).

20. **SHABACH (King James Version)**

commend, glory, keep in, praise, still, triumph.

21. **SHABACH (Brown-Driver-Briggs' definition)**

(1) to soothe, to still, to stroke (a) (Piel) to soothe, to still (b) (Hiphil) stilling (participle) (2) to laud, to praise, to commend (a) (Piel) (1) to laud, to praise (God) (2) to commend, to congratulate (the dead) (b) (Hithpael) to boast.

The word means "to shout, address in a loud tone, to commend." It is the exclamatory form of praise. The particular word for "shout" is translated "praise" only a few times:

THE DIFFERENCE BETWEEN PRAISE AND WORSHIP

Because thy lovingkindness is better than life, my lips shall praise thee.

Psalm 63:3

O praise the LORD, all ye nations: praise him, all ye people.

Psalm 117:1

One generation shall praise thy works to another, and shall declare thy mighty acts.

Psalm 145:4

Praise the LORD, O Jerusalem; praise thy God, O Zion.

Psalm 147:12

The word corresponding to SHEBACH is *Shabach* and is used in connection with praise three places in Daniel. On the first occasion Daniel testified:

I thank thee, and praise thee, O thou God of my fathers, who hast given me wisdom and might, and hast made known unto me now what we desired of thee: for thou hast now made known unto us the king's matter.

Daniel 2:23

The other two cases have to do with Nebuchadnezzar's restoration to sanity.

And at the end of the days I Nebuchadnezzar lifted up mine eyes unto heaven, and mine understanding returned unto me, and I blessed the most High, and I praised and honoured him that liveth for ever, whose dominion is an everlasting dominion, and his kingdom is from generation to generation:

Daniel 4:34

Further, he testifies in Daniel 4:37:

Now I Nebuchadnezzar praise and extol and honour the King of heaven, all whose works are truth, and his ways judgment: and those that walk in pride he is able to abase.

SUMMARY OF SEVEN HEBREW PRAISE WORDS:

HALLAL	To laud, boast, rave, celebrate
YADAH	To praise with extended hands; to throw out the hands
BARAK	To bless
TEHILLAH	To sing or laud; derived from Hallal and is generally accepted to mean "the singing of Hallals"
ZAMAR	To pluck the strings of an instrument to praise with song
TOWDAH	To extend the hands in thanksgiving, a thank-offering
SHABACH	To commend, address in a loud tone, to shout; an exclamatory form of praise in a special sense

OTHER HEBREW WORDS FOR PRAISE

Only the 7 principle words in the Hebrew language have been covered thus far. There are many others connected with praise which refer to the action involved but do not use the word "praise" and are used with the exercise of praise.

ANAH	Testify (sing)
ALATZ	Rejoice
GADAL	Magnify, praise
GIL	Shout, circle in joy
HILLUL	Celebration of thanksgiving (for harvest)
HAPHETZ	Delight, take pleasure in
HUL	Dance

THE DIFFERENCE BETWEEN PRAISE AND WORSHIP

HAVAH	Worship, kneel, prostrate
HADAH	Rejoice
KAVED	Honor, glorify
KARAR	Dance
MIZMOR	Psalm
MAHA	Clap
MAHOL	Dance (noun)
MEHOLAH	Dance (noun)
NEGINAH	Music, song, stringed instrument
NASA	Lift (voice)
NATAN	Proclaim, strike, give
PAAR	Boast, glorify
PAZAZ	Leap
PATZAH	Burst forth with
QARA	Proclaim, call
RUM	Exalt, extol
RUA	Shout in triumph
RINNAH	Shout of joy
RANAN	Shout with joy
RAQAD	Dance, skip about
SELAL	Exalt, sing
SAPHAR	Recount, proclaim
SUS	Rejoice
SAHAQ	Play, dance
SAMAH	Rejoice, be glad
SHAVAH	Glorify, praise
SHIR	Sing
SHAMA	Proclaim
TZAHAL	Shout for joy
ZAKAR	Remember, acknowledge, praise
ZAMIR	Song
ZIMRAH	Song

Note: The above words are translated "praise" in the New International Version.

PRAISE— A WORD STUDY IN GREEK

As in Hebrew there are several words translated "praise" but many more connected with praise, so it is in Greek. First let's deal with those words which are commonly translated "praise" and observe their usages. We will observe them alphabetically.

1.   **AINESIS, AINOS, AINEO (Strong's definition) (ahee-neh'-o)**

to praise (God)

2.   **AINEO (King James Version)**

praise

3.   **AINEO (Thayer's definition)**

(1) to praise, to extol, to sing praises in honor to God (2) to allow, to recommend (3) to promise or vow

The first two are nouns, the last a verb, and all are related. They are words used only in praise to God. In the Septuagint, the first five books of the Old Testament, in Greek AINEO corresponds to HALLAL and YADAH, the commonest of the Hebrew words for praise. It is translated "praise" in every usage in the King James Version. The usages are listed as follows:

> And suddenly there was with the angel a multitude of the heavenly host praising God, and saying,
> Luke 2:13

> And the shepherds returned, glorifying and praising God for all the things that they had heard and seen, as it was told unto them.
> Luke 2:20

> And immediately he received his sight, and followed him, glorifying God: and all the people, when they saw it, gave praise unto God.
> Luke 18:43

And said unto him, Hearest thou what these say? And Jesus saith unto them, Yea; have ye never read, Out of the mouth of babes and sucklings thou hast perfected praise?

Matthew 21:16

And when he was come nigh, even now at the descent of the mount of Olives, the whole multitude of the disciples began to rejoice and praise God with a loud voice for all the mighty works that they had seen;

Luke 19:37

And were continually in the temple, praising and blessing God. Amen.

Luke 24:53

Praising God, and having favour with all the people. And the Lord added to the church daily such as should be saved.
Acts 2:47

And he leaping up stood, and walked, and entered with them into the temple, walking, and leaping, and praising God.

And all the people saw him walking and praising God:

Acts 3:8-9

And again, Praise the Lord, all ye Gentiles; and laud him, all ye people.

Romans 15:11

By him therefore let us offer the sacrifice of praise to God continually, that is, the fruit of our lips giving thanks to his name.

Hebrews 13:15

4. **DOXA (noun), DOXAZO (verb) (Strong's definition) (dox'-ah)**

   glory (as very apparent), in a wide application (literal or figurative, objective or subjective)

5. **DOXA (King James Version)**

    dignity, glory (-ious), honor, praise, worship

6. **DOXA (Thayer's definition)**

    (1) an opinion, a judgment, a view (2) an opinion, an estimate, whether good or bad concerning someone in the New Testament, always a good opinion concerning one, resulting in praise, honor, and glory (3) splendor, brightness (a) used of the moon, sun, stars (b) magnificence, excellence, preeminence, dignity, grace (c) majesty (1) a thing belonging to God; the kingly majesty which belongs to Him as supreme ruler, majesty in the sense of the absolute perfection of the deity (2) a thing belonging to Christ (a) the kingly majesty of the Messiah (b) the absolutely perfect inward or personal excellency of Christ; the majesty (3) used of the angels; as apparent in their exterior brightness (4) a most glorious condition, most exalted state (a) used of that condition with God the Father in heaven to which Christ was raised after He had achieved his work on earth (b) the glorious condition of blessedness into which is appointed and promised that true Christians shall enter after their Savior's return from heaven

The word DOXA and its verb DOXAZO are generally translated "glory" and "glorify" respectively. The New International Version sometimes translates it "praise" in both noun and verb form. It comes from a word meaning "to seem or suppose." It signifies an opinion, estimate or an honor resulting from good opinion. Whether translated "glory" or "praise," it is a good word in ascribing to God the honor due Him. Let's look at some New Testament references:

> Glory to God in the highest, and on earth peace, good will toward men.
>
> Luke 2:14

> And immediately he received his sight, and followed him, glorifying God: and all the people, when they saw it, gave praise unto God.
>
> Luke 18:43

THE DIFFERENCE BETWEEN PRAISE AND WORSHIP

And immediately the angel of the Lord smote him, because he gave not God the glory: and he was eaten of worms, and gave up the ghost.

Acts 12:23

It is interesting to observe that Herod was smitten with worms and died when he refused to give praise (doza) to God. Paul, in recounting Abraham's faith, said in Romans 4:20:

He staggered not at the promise of God through unbelief; but was strong in faith, giving glory to God;

Our word "doxology" is taken from the word "doxa." A famous doxology is found in Romans 11:36:

For of him, and through him, and to him, are all things: to whom be glory for ever. Amen.

Common forms of praise are found in:

To whom be glory for ever and ever. Amen.
Galatians 1:5

Now unto God and our Father be glory for ever and ever. Amen.

Philippians 4:20

If any man speak, let him speak as the oracles of God; if any man minister, let him do it as of the ability which God giveth: that God in all things may be glorified through Jesus Christ, to whom be praise and dominion for ever and ever. Amen.
1 Peter 4:11

But grow in grace, and in the knowledge of our Lord and Saviour Jesus Christ. To him be glory both now and for ever. Amen.

II Peter 3:18

Please note the concluding statement on DOXAZO in W.E. Vine's Expository Dictionary of New Testament words is too good to leave out. He says "As the glory of God is the revelation of all that He is and has. It is said of a self-revelation in which God manifests all that is His.

> **Father, glorify thy name. Then came there a voice from heaven, saying, I have both glorified it, and will glorify it again.**
> **John 12:28**

So far it is Christ through whom this is made manifest. He is said to glorify (*doxazo*) the Father, or the Father is glorified in Him; and Christ's meaning is analogous when He says to His disciples "Herein is my Father glorified, that ye bear much fruit; and so shall ye be my disciples." When DOXAZO is predicated on Christ, it simply means that His innate glory is brought to the light, is made manifest. As the revelation of the Holy Spirit is connected with the glorification of Christ, Christ says regarding Him "He shall glorify (*doxazo*) me."

7. **EPAINOS (noun), EPAINEO (verb)**
   (Strong's definition) (ep'-ahee-nos);

   laudation; concretely, a commendable thing

8. **EPAINOS (King James Version)**

   praise

9. **EPAINOS (Thayer's definition)**

   approbation, commendation, praise

This is the word for praise (*anios*) with the preposition *epi*. W.E. Vine indicates that this is a strengthened form of *ainos*. This word is also used in reference to man praising man. There are nine references in the New

THE DIFFERENCE BETWEEN PRAISE AND WORSHIP

Testament which involves EPAINOS relating to our study of praise, They are as follows:

But he is a Jew, which is one inwardly; and circumcision is that of the heart, in the spirit, and not in the letter; whose praise is not of men, but of God.

Romans 2:29

For rulers are not a terror to good works, but to the evil. Wilt thou then not be afraid of the power? Do that which is good, and thou shalt have praise of the same:

Romans 13:3

Therefore judge nothing before the time, until the Lord come, who both will bring to light the hidden things of darkness, and will make manifest the counsels of the hearts: and then shall every man have praise of God.

1 Corinthians 4:5

Having predestinated us unto the adoption of children by Jesus Christ to himself, according to the good pleasure of his will,

To the praise of the glory of his grace, wherein he hath made us accepted in the beloved.

Ephesians 1:5-6

That we should be to the praise of his glory, who first trusted in Christ.

Ephesians 1:12

Which is the earnest of our inheritance until the redemption of the purchased possession, unto the praise of his glory.

Ephesians 1:14

Being filled with the fruits of righteousness, which are by Jesus Christ, unto the glory and praise of God.

Philippians 1:11

That the trial of your faith, being much more precious than of gold that perisheth, though it be tried with fire, might be found unto praise and honour and glory at the appearing of Jesus Christ:

1 Peter 1:7

10. **EULOGATOS, EULOGIA (Strong's definition)**
    eulogetos (yoo-log-ay-tos')

    adorable

11. **EULOGATOS (King James Version)**

    blessed

12. **EULOGETOS (Thayer's definition)**

    blessed, praised

This is a word that is never used of man, only of God. It means "blessed" or "praised." The word in Hebrew that corresponds to this is *baruk* or *barak* generally translated "blessed or blessing, or bless." Zachariah, at the birth of his son John the Baptist, was filled with the Holy Spirit and began his first utterance with praise saying, "Blessed be the Lord God of Israel; for he hath visited and redeemed his people." (Luke 1:68)

Our English word is a transliteration of the Greek word "eulogia." The eulogy involves commendation and praise. Paul reminds us that God is ever being praised (eulogatos). Other uses of these words are as follows:

> **Blessed be God, even the Father of our Lord Jesus Christ, the Father of mercies, and the God of all comfort;**
>
> 2 Corinthians 1:3

> **Blessed be the God and Father of our Lord Jesus Christ, who hath blessed us with all spiritual blessings in heavenly places in Christ:**
>
> Ephesians 1:3

THE DIFFERENCE BETWEEN PRAISE AND WORSHIP

Blessed be the God and Father of our Lord Jesus Christ, who hath blessed us with all spiritual blessings in heavenly places in Christ:

Ephesians 1:3

Blessed be the God and Father of our Lord Jesus Christ, which according to his abundant mercy hath begotten us again unto a lively hope by the resurrection of Jesus Christ from the dead,

1 Peter 1:3

Out of the same mouth proceedeth blessing and cursing. My brethren, these things ought not so to be.

James 3:10

Saying with a loud voice, Worthy is the Lamb that was slain to receive power, and riches, and wisdom, and strength, and honour, and glory, and blessing.

And every creature which is in heaven, and on the earth, and under the earth, and such as are in the sea, and all that are in them, heard I saying, Blessing, and honour, and glory, and power, be unto him that sitteth upon the throne, and unto the Lamb for ever and ever.

Revelation 5:12-13

Saying, Amen: Blessing, and glory, and wisdom, and thanksgiving, and honour, and power, and might, be unto our God for ever and ever. Amen.

Revelation 7:12

Isn't it wonderful that we are capable of blessing the Lord with words! Out of that God-given ability will come the joy of blessing others as well.

13. **EXOMOLOGEMAI (Strong's definition)**
    exomologeo (ex-om-ol-og-eh'-o)

    to acknowledge or (by implication of assent) agree fully

14. **EXOMOLOGEMAI (King James Version)**

   to confess, profess, promise

15. **EXOMOLOGEO (Thayer's definition)**

   (1) to confess (2) to profess (a) to acknowledge openly and joyfully (b) to one's honor: to celebrate, give praise to (c) to profess that one will do something, to promise, to agree, to engage

   This is derivative of *homologeo* which means "to confess." The preposition *ek* which means "out of" makes the word stronger and more intense. It may be taken to mean "to confess openly and freely." It is translated "praise" or "thank" three times in the King James Version, two of which are utterances from the lips of Jesus.

   > At that time Jesus answered and said, I thank thee, O Father, Lord of heaven and earth, because thou hast hid these things from the wise and prudent, and hast revealed them unto babes.
   >
   > Matthew 11:25

   > In that hour Jesus rejoiced in spirit, and said, I thank thee, O Father, Lord of heaven and earth, that thou hast hid these things from the wise and prudent, and hast revealed them unto babes: even so, Father; for so it seemed good in thy sight.
   >
   > Luke 10:21

16. **HUMNEO, HUMNOS (Strong's definition) (hoom-neh'-o)**

   to hymn, i.e., sing a religious ode; by implication, to celebrate (God) in song:

17. **HUMNEO (King James Version)**

   sing a hymn (praise unto)

18. **HUMNEO (Thayer's definition)**

(1) to sing the praise of, to sing hymns to (2) to sing a hymn, to sing; singing of paschal hymns (Psalms 113-118 and 136), which the Jews called the "great Hallel"

This word simply means "to sing praise." Only once is it translated "praise."

> Saying, I will declare thy name unto my brethren, in the midst of the church will I sing praise unto thee.
>
> Hebrews 2:12

Other uses are in ...

> And when they had sung an hymn, they went out into the mount of Olives.
>
> Matthew 26:30

> And he said, So is the kingdom of God, as if a man should cast seed into the ground;
>
> Mark 4:26

> And at midnight Paul and Silas prayed, and sang praises unto God: and the prisoners heard them.
>
> Acts 16:25

> Speaking to yourselves in psalms and hymns and spiritual songs, singing and making melody in your heart to the Lord;
>
> Ephesians 5:19

> Let the word of Christ dwell in you richly in all wisdom; teaching and admonishing one another in psalms and hymns and spiritual songs, singing with grace in your hearts to the Lord.
>
> Colossians 3:16

There is another reference to praise which must be mentioned. Reference has already been made to

> **But ye are a chosen generation, a royal priesthood, an holy nation, a peculiar people; that ye should shew forth the praises of him who hath called you out of darkness into his marvellous light:**
>
> 1 Peter 2:9

The phrase "proclaim the praises of Him" uses two Greek words. The first is *exangelo* which means "to proclaim or put out a message." *Angelos* is used with reference to angels or messengers. The other word is *arate* which means virtue or praise.

19. **MEGALUNO (Strong's definition) (meg-al-oo'-no)**

    to make (or declare) great, i.e. increase or (figuratively) extol:

20. **MEGALUNO (King James Version)**

    enlarge, magnify, shew great

21. **MEGALUNO (Thayer's definition)**

    (1) to make great, to magnify; metaphorically, to make conspicuous (2) to deem or to declare great; to esteem highly, to extol, to laud, to celebrate (3) to get glory and praise

This word means "make great, large, or long; or to magnify." The King James Version renders this word "magnify" in the following 3 instances:

> **And Mary said, My soul doth magnify the Lord,**
>
> Luke 1:46

For they heard them speak with tongues, and magnify God. Then answered Peter,

Acts 10:46

And this was known to all the Jews and Greeks also dwelling at Ephesus; and fear fell on them all, and the name of the Lord Jesus was magnified.

Acts 19:17

The definite connotation in all three instances is "praise." *Megaluno* is the word which corresponds to the Hebrew word *gadal* which means "extol."

22. **PSALLO (verb) PSALMOS (noun) (Strong's definition) (psal'-lo)**

    probably strengthened from *psao* (to rub or touch the surface); to twitch or twang, i.e. to play on a stringed instrument (celebrate the divine worship with music and accompanying odes)

23. **PSALLO (King James Version)**

    (to) make melody, sing (psalms)

24. **PSALLO (Thayer's definition)**

    (1) to pluck off, to pull out (2) to cause to vibrate by touching, to twang (a) to touch or to strike the chord, to twang the strings of a musical instrument so that they gently vibrate (b) to play on a stringed instrument, to play, the harp, etc. (c) in the Septuagint, to sing with the music of the harp (d) in the New Testament, to sing a hymn, to celebrate the praises of God in song

This word means to sing praise in spiritual ecstasy or to make melody. The most significant fact about this word in the light of this study is that in the Septuagint it is the Greek rendering of the word *Zamar*, meaning "to sing or to pluck the strings of an instrument" some 40 times. It is also used 10 times for the Hebrew word *Ranan* meaning "to shout for joy." The noun *psalmos* simply means a song of praise.

The 4 uses in the New Testament are:

And that the Gentiles might glorify God for his mercy; as it is written, For this cause I will confess to thee among the Gentiles, and sing unto thy name.

Romans 15:9

What is it then? I will pray with the spirit, and I will pray with the understanding also: I will sing with the spirit, and I will sing with the understanding also.

1 Corinthians 14:15

Speaking to yourselves in psalms and hymns and spiritual songs, singing and making melody in your heart to the Lord;

Ephesians 5:19

Is any among you afflicted? Let him pray. Is any merry? Let him sing psalms.

James 5:13

OTHER GREEK WORDS FOR PRAISE

The following are several other Greek words translated as praise:

AGALLIO	Exult, be glad
ADO	Sing
ALLOMAI	Leap
ANTHOMOLOGEOMAI	Praise, thanks
GONUPETEPO	Kneel down
EUPHRAINO	Rejoice
EUCHARISTEO	Gives thanks
EUCHARISTIA	Thanksgiving
EUCHARISTOS	Thankful

THE DIFFERENCE BETWEEN PRAISE AND WORSHIP

KAMPTO	To bend the knee
KAUCHAOMAI	To boast
PIPTO	To fall to the ground
PROSKUNEO	To fall down and worship
SKIRTAO	To leap with joy
SUNADOMAI	To rejoice
CHAIRO	To rejoice
CHARIS	Thanks, grace
ODA	Song
HOSANNA	Save Lord

WHAT IS PRAISE?

It has been said that it is perhaps the greatest need for all Christendom to have a clear understanding of Biblical teaching on the subject for praise and worship. There is no doubt from the history of the Bible and church history that generations that failed to praise failed in every other area, and the world is suffering because of its failure to praise.

Praise is crucial to our relationship to Father God and our testimony to the world. There is too much to lose if we decide to ignore it, not only to the church but to world also. The church will perish through lack of knowledge of it, and much of the world will be destroyed which could have been evangelized through praise and worship.

PRAISE IS LIFE

Praise is not something we do "for fun;" it's something we do to live. Praise is life: it's the life of the church, it's the life of man, and in these last days it will be life to a dying world. Praise gets the attention of men and God and when man "sees" God, he gets saved.

The following scriptures testify to the fact that praise is a sign of life:

The dead praise not the LORD, neither any that go down into silence.

But we will bless the LORD from this time forth and for evermore. Praise the LORD.

Psalm 115:17-18

We know that the dead in Christ praise the Lord and this will be our eternal occupation. These scriptures are not talking about them; they are drawing a comparison to those who are dead to Christ not being able to praise Him, in comparison to we who will praise Him now and forever. In other words, praise is sign of life. Those who are redeemed by the Blood of Jesus should evidence the life of God in them by their praise.

What profit is there in my blood, when I go down to the pit? Shall the dust praise thee? Shall it declare thy truth?

Psalm 30:9

The implication here is "what profit is there in death?" The life is gone out of the body and the body cannot praise because the blood has gone back to dust. The good news is that the Blood of Jesus that was shed has secured life for us, and we will praise with our glorified bodies forever. The grave is no threat to us— our praise goes on eternally.

For the grave cannot praise thee, death can not celebrate thee: they that go down into the pit cannot hope for thy truth.

The living, the living, he shall praise thee, as I do this day: the father to the children shall make known thy truth.

Isaiah 38:18-19

There is no praise for anyone who goes to hell, because there is no hope for them in any way. The tragedy is that those who die outside of Christ will never sing. Singing was birthed in God and eternal separation from Him causes the song to die. I am convinced that there will be no song in hell and no music because there is nothing to sing about. Only then will the reality of God hit many who have rejected Jesus all their lives as they go from a world full of music and song to a place of silence. In contrast, the believer goes into a musical extravaganza, not only for a moment but forever ....

> **Let the sinners be consumed out of the earth, and let the wicked be no more. Bless thou the LORD, O my soul. Praise ye the LORD.**
>
> Psalm 104:35

> **While I live will I praise the LORD: I will sing praises unto my God while I have any being.**
>
> Psalm 146:2

The Psalms of Israel and, generally speaking, the Word of God does not speak of a life of faith where there is no praise to God. Praise then, is simply the evidence of the life of God in you and me.

TEHILLAH PRAISE

> **Enter into his gates with thanksgiving, and into his courts with praise: be thankful unto him, and bless his name.**
>
> Psalm 100:4

This is the high praise of God: it is the praise that God inhabits. Jesus takes us into the place where God lives, but we must still praise so that God will inhabit our praise. We might well be in the place where God lives (salvation) but never experience the manifestation of God or the real presence of God because we are reluctant to praise. TEHILLAH praise is praise that implies that our God has responded to our faith. Whilst other forms of praise involve faith, TEHILLAH praise is suggesting that God has responded to our faith to the extent that He literally inhabits and is enthroned in the midst of it.

> But thou art holy, O thou that inhabitest the praises of Israel.
>
> Psalm 22:3

> For the grave cannot praise thee, death can not celebrate thee: they that go down into the pit cannot hope for thy truth.
>
> The living, the living, he shall praise thee, as I do this day: the father to the children shall make known thy truth.
>
> Isaiah 38:18-19

> What profit is there in my blood, when I go down to the pit? Shall the dust praise thee? Shall it declare thy truth?
>
> Psalm 30:9

> The dead praise not the LORD, neither any that go down into silence.
>
> Psalm 115:17

Praise is a sign of life; inside the walls of salvation there is life, so there must be praise in a Christian's experience if he truly wants to be alive to God. Outside the walls there is no life, only death and obviously no praise. Praise in a Christian's life is a good indication of his "distance" to or from God. If he is far off from God (although he is still saved), you can be sure that he will not be a praiser. If he is close to God, praise is something he continually does because it's the natural response to intimacy with God.

Let's note that thanksgiving involves mostly man giving to God. Praise, excluding TEHILLAH, requires more faith than we use for thanksgiving. The very fact that we are operating in these praise realms indicates that we have studied them in God's Word and faith to do them has come by hearing. Again, it is mostly action from man to God.

TEHILLAH praise, however, according to the Word, is praise that God inhabits and here we see action not only from man's side, but from God's side, i.e., man praises and God inhabits. This does require greater faith— it is faith in action to the fullest. Note: TEHILLAH takes us over to another realm: the realm of God inhabiting our praise. When God inhabits our praise, we don't have to exercise faith to believe for anything. God is in our midst. We don't need faith. The Bible does not indicate that we will need faith in heaven to worship God because we are in His presence there. No faith is needed when that which you have been believing for is manifest.

Worship involves no faith because, in true worship, God is already in our midst and in that place we are sitting on His lap. We are not believing to get there; we are already there. It is, as it were, God Who has come to us. Worship is a realm when the Holy Spirit has taken over.

SUMMARY

Praise— You cannot separate faith and praise, except when praise becomes worship. Worship is enjoying the intimacy of the Father that praise has produced.

Worship— Why no faith? Because we see Him clearly, vividly for who He is. We understand His attributes; we know His ways. In worship we don't respond to God for what He has done or what He is going to do for us. We simply love Him for who He is.

Now faith is the substance of things hoped for, the evidence of things not seen.

Hebrews 11:1

A true worshipper is not hoping to see God; he sees Him. A true worshipper is not hoping to love God; he loves Him.

I am not saying that you don't have to have faith to worship God. I am saying that great faith will take you through high praise to a place where you don't have to exercise faith to love God, and that place is worship. At this place of worship our faith has already done its work. I also don't want to give you the impression that we have to laboriously go through six steps of praise to get TEHILLAH before we can get to worship. No! That would be works. I am saying, however, that a worshipper is a person who was and still is a person of faith.

> **Now the just shall live by faith: but if any man draw back, my soul shall have no pleasure in him**
>
> **Hebrews 10:38**

> **But without faith it is impossible to please him: for he that cometh to God must believe that he is, and that he is a rewarder of them that diligently seek him.**
>
> **Hebrews 11:6**

Only by continually exercising our faith will we stay in that place of worship, because it took faith to get us there and will require faith to keep us there. The worshipper will continually be aware of personal faith and be totally dependent upon it, although at the place of worship his personal faith has done its work.

WHY SHOULD WE PRAISE?

We praise because the One who loves us has commanded us to. There is no option, but God will never force us to praise if don't want to. The Bible is a book that is basically saying one thing: LOVE GOD. How do we express our love to God? In praise and worship. We can talk about missions and evangelism, teachers and pastors, fruits and gifts of the Spirit, but it all comes back to two individuals face to face. One is God and the other is man, and the question that is asked is "how much do you love Me?" Guess who asks the question? If you and I are still at the place where we are asking God how much He loves us, then we need salvation because we know nothing of Jesus.

If we are at the place where we are questioning God's actions and motives, then we don't know Him and praise is far from us. But if we are at the place where we know His love and know that all His actions and motives are good for us, then we are in a position to praise.

THE DIFFERENCE BETWEEN PRAISE AND WORSHIP

We should praise God because it is a natural response. We are not commanded to breathe, we just do it. Praise should be the same. If we have to think about why we should praise, then we have not gotten pass the understanding of salvation. God has recreated us to praise His name, and we see this in the following passages.

NEW TESTAMENT REASONS WHY WE SHOULD PRAISE GOD

To the praise of the glory of his grace, wherein he hath made us accepted in the beloved.
Ephesians 1:6, 12, 14

That we should be to the praise of his glory, who first trusted in Christ.

Which is the earnest of our inheritance until the redemption of the purchased possession, unto the praise of his glory.

The Triune Godhead is at work on our behalf so that we may display praise to their glory. The Eternal Triune Godhead has acted in such knowledge, wisdom, compassion, mercy, holiness, justice, righteousness, grace, and love to His own that we, the objects of these excellencies, must respond to Him in praise. As one reflects on the love the Father, the wonder of Jesus, and the presence of the Holy Spirit, praise is the necessary outflow.

Many reasons are given in scriptures as to why we should praise and some taken from the Old Testament are listed below:

SOME OLD TESTAMENT REASONS WHY WE SHOULD PRAISE GOD

Psa. 95:6-7	Because He is our God and we are His people
Psa. 9:4	As a testimony to His people
Psa. 18:3; 48:1; 47:6	He is worthy and great and a King
Psa. 50:23	To glorify Him

THE MECHANICS OF TRUE WORSHIP

Psa. 63:3-4; 107:8	Because His loving kindness is better than life and because of His goodness
Psa. 67:3-4; 97:11	Because of His righteous judgements
Psa. 92:1-4; 135:3	It is a good thing to give thanks and to sing praises
Psa. 102:18	We are created to praise the Lord
Psa. 5:11	Because He defends us
Psa. 13:6	He has dealt bountifully with us
Psa. 27:6; 28:7; 31:7	He lifted my head above my enemies and He is my strength and my shield
Psa. 33:1	Praise is comely
Psa. 33:3-4; 52:9	Because His word is right and He has done it
Psa. 69:34-35	For God will save Zion and build Judah
Psa. 86:10-13; 96:3-4	For His mercy is great and He is great
Psa. 89:5-6; 99:9	For there is none like our God, He is holy
Psa. 135:3	For He is good
Psa. 3:3	My glory
Psa. 3:3; 113:7	My lifter
Psa.18:2; 31:3	He is our Fortress
Psa. 18:3-4	He is our Buckler
Psa. 18:2; 61:3	He is our High Tower
Psa. 16:7; 37:23	He gives us counsel
Psa.68:5	He is Father to the fatherless
Psa.5:11; 31:2	He is my Defender
Psa. 8:1;148:13	His name is Excellent
Psa. 9:4	For righteous judgements
Psa. 9:14; 18:46	Salvation
Psa.18:1; 27:1; 28:7	He is my strength
Psa. 86:10; 98:1	For He has done wondrous works
Psa. 89:1,5,8	For His great Faithfulness
Psa. 99:3,5,9	For He is holy
Psa. 95:3; 89:6,8	For He is above all other gods
Psa.95:6	For He is our Maker
Psa. 103:3	He forgives
Psa. 103:3	He heals all our diseases
Psa. 103:5; 107:9	He satisfies

THE DIFFERENCE BETWEEN PRAISE AND WORSHIP

Psa. 106:1; 136; 117:2	For His mercy endureth forever
Psa. 111:2; 126:2	He does great works
Psa. 116:1	He hears my voice
Psa. 116:5	He is gracious
Psa. 135:3; 147:1	It is pleasant to sing praise
Psa. 139	God understands us, He made us
Psa. 142:7	He has brought me out of prison
Psa. 144:1	He has taught my fingers to fight war

CHAPTER VI

TO WHOM SHOULD WE DIRECT OUR PRAISE?

Though the word "Trinity" is not mentioned in the scriptures, the triunity of the Godhead is clearly evident in the scriptures. The eternal Godhead is revealed as consisting of three persons, each equal and eternal with each other; The Father, the Son and the Holy Spirit. Each person of the Godhead possesses a distinct personality, yet these three are but one in essence. There are not three gods, but one Godhead revealed in three persons. There is no jealousy in the Eternal Godhead because each person delights to glorify the other.

The Holy Spirit is equal to the Father and the Son and the Scripture clearly points out in many instances where the Holy Spirit is called the Spirit of God and also the Spirit of Christ.

> **But ye are not in the flesh, but in the Spirit, if so be that the Spirit of God dwell in you. Now if any man have not the Spirit of Christ, he is none of his.**
>
> **Romans 8:9**

The Holy Spirit is the revelation of God the Father and God the Son, and He calls us to the Son, and the Son calls us to the Father. Regarding praising the Godhead as individuals, we can only look to Scripture for the answer. To do this we will look at the members of the Trinity individually.

THE HOLY SPIRIT

We are not instructed to worship the Holy Spirit. There is no precept, or example in Scripture either for addressing the Holy Spirit personally in prayer, or of directly offering praise to Him. We are instructed to pray in the Spirit (by the Holy Spirit), but not to Him.

> **Praying always with all prayer and supplication in the Spirit, and watching thereunto with all perseverance and supplication for all saints;**
>
> **Ephesians 6:18**

> But the hour cometh, and now is, when the true worshippers shall worship the Father in spirit and in truth: for the Father seeketh such to worship him.
>
> John 4:23

It must be understood that without the work of the Holy Spirit in our lives we could neither pray nor worship as we ought. The Holy Spirit makes these possible to the believer.

In relationship to praise and worship, the Holy Spirit leads and guides the individual believer through the Word of God to an ever-increasing apprehension and appreciation of the Father and the Son. As the believer is taught by the Holy Spirit through the Word, and is obedient to what he learns, the Spirit will lead him on to a deeper knowledge of Divine things and particularly in the area of praise and worship. It is the Spirit that gives us the confidence to come into God's presence and cry "Abba, Father." It is in the Holy Spirit's power and presence that we have access to worship.

THE FATHER (GOD)

> That all men should honour the Son, even as they honour the Father. He that honoureth not the Son honoureth not the Father which hath sent him.
>
> John 5:23

The word "honour" implies worship and we see from this scripture that we cannot worship the Father without worshipping the Son, and vice versa. It is more meaningful than that and infers that we cannot worship the Father unless we worship the Son, and we cannot worship the Son unless we worship the Father.

> And Thomas answered and said unto him, My Lord and my God.
>
> John 20:28

Jesus laid a solid foundation in John 4 when He informed the Samaritan woman about worshipping the Father. He is carefully identifying

TO WHOM SHOULD WE DIRECT OUR PRAISE?

the object of true worship: the Father God, and we know that we can only go to the Father God through Jesus. Acceptable worship to the Father is only accessible through His precious Son, Jesus.

> Jesus saith unto him, I am the way, the truth, and the life: no man cometh unto the Father, but by me.
>
> If ye had known me, ye should have known my Father also: and from henceforth ye know him, and have seen him.
>
> John 14:6-7

REASONS WHY WE SHOULD WORSHIP THE FATHER

BECAUSE OF WHAT HE IS

The Holy Father	Joh. 17:11; Heb. 1:9
The Righteous Father	Joh.17:25
The Father of Glory	Eph.1:17
The Father of Lights	Jam.1:17; Joh.1:5; Eph.5:13
The Father of Mercies	2Cor.1:13; Psa.103:13; 107:1
The Father of All	Eph.4:6
The Father of our Lord Jesus Christ	2Cor.1:3; Eph.1:3; 1Pet.1:3; 1Tim. 3:16

BECAUSE OF WHAT HE HAS DONE

He has loved us	Joh.3:16
Eternal love	Jer. 31:3
Revealed love	Joh.3:16
Manifested love	1Joh.4:9
Bestowed love	1Joh. 3:1
Inseparable love	Rom. 8:38-39
He has given us His Son	Joh.3:16
He has chosen us in Christ	Eph. 1:3-4
He has saved us by His Grace	Col.1:12-13

He has blessed us   Eph.1:3
He has made us His Children   1Joh.3:1
He has made it possible for us to worship   Joh.4:23-24

THE SON (JESUS CHRIST)

Apart from the foundation we have already laid showing the Son to be co-equal, co-eternal, and co-existing with the Father and therefore worthy of the same worship, there are some specific scriptures that refer to worshipping Jesus.

WORSHIP BY ANGELS

And again, when he bringeth in the firstbegotten into the world, he saith, And let all the angels of God worship him.

Hebrews 1:6

WORSHIP IN THE FUTURE

That at the name of Jesus every knee should bow, of things in heaven, and things in earth, and things under the earth;

Philippians 2:10

WORSHIP IN HEAVEN

And when he had taken the book, the four beasts and four and twenty elders fell down before the Lamb, having every one of them harps, and golden vials full of odours, which are the prayers of saints.

And they sung a new song, saying, Thou art worthy to take the book, and to open the seals thereof: for thou wast slain, and hast redeemed us to God by thy blood out of every kindred, and tongue, and people, and nation;

TO WHOM SHOULD WE DIRECT OUR PRAISE?

And hast made us unto our God kings and priests: and we shall reign on the earth.

And I beheld, and I heard the voice of many angels round about the throne and the beasts and the elders: and the number of them was ten thousand times ten thousand, and thousands of thousands;

Saying with a loud voice, Worthy is the Lamb that was slain to receive power, and riches, and wisdom, and strength, and honour, and glory, and blessing.

And every creature which is in heaven, and on the earth, and under the earth, and such as are in the sea, and all that are in them, heard I saying, Blessing, and honour, and glory, and power, be unto him that sitteth upon the throne, and unto the Lamb for ever and ever.

Revelation 5:8-13

Note the following scriptures which refer also to Jesus being worshipped by man at various stages:

AT BIRTH

And when they were come into the house, they saw the young child with Mary his mother, and fell down, and worshipped him: and when they had opened their treasures, they presented unto him gifts; gold, and frankincense, and myrrh.

Matthew 2:11

DURING HIS MINISTRY

And, behold, there came a leper and worshipped him, saying, Lord, if thou wilt, thou canst make me clean.

Matthew 8:2

While he spake these things unto them, behold, there came a certain ruler, and worshipped him, saying, My daughter is even now dead: but come and lay thy hand upon her, and she shall live.

            Matthew 9:18

Then they that were in the ship came and worshipped him, saying, Of a truth thou art the Son of God.

            Matthew 14:33

Then came she and worshipped him, saying, Lord, help me.

            Matthew 15:25

AT HIS RESURRECTION

And as they went to tell his disciples, behold, Jesus met them, saying, All hail. And they came and held him by the feet, and worshipped him.

And when they saw him, they worshipped him: but some doubted.

            Matthew 28:9,17

AT HIS ASCENSION

And they worshipped him, and returned to Jerusalem with great joy:

            Luke 24:52

REASONS WHY THE SON SHOULD BE WORSHIPPED

BECAUSE OF WHO HE IS:

THE SON OF GOD

In the beginning was the Word, and the Word was with God, and the Word was God.

> John 1:1

THE CREATOR OF ALL THINGS

For by him were all things created, that are in heaven, and that are in earth, visible and invisible, whether they be thrones, or dominions, or principalities, or powers: all things were created by him, and for him:

> Colossians 1:16

All things were made by him; and without him was not any thing made that was made.

> John 1:3

BECAUSE HE IS THE REVEALER OF THE FATHER

No man hath seen God at any time; the only begotten Son, which is in the bosom of the Father, he hath declared him.

> John 1:18

Jesus saith unto him, I am the way, the truth, and the life: no man cometh unto the Father, but by me.

If ye had known me, ye should have known my Father also: and from henceforth ye know him, and have seen him.

Philip saith unto him, Lord, shew us the Father, and it sufficeth us.

Jesus saith unto him, Have I been so long time with you, and yet hast thou not known me, Philip? He that hath seen me hath seen the Father; and how sayest thou then, Shew us the Father?

Believest thou not that I am in the Father, and the Father in me? The words that I speak unto you I speak not of myself: but the Father that dwelleth in me, he doeth the works.

Believe me that I am in the Father, and the Father in me: or else believe me for the very works' sake.

John 14:6-11

Who being the brightness of his glory, and the express image of his person, and upholding all things by the word of his power, when he had by himself purged our sins, sat down on the right hand of the Majesty on high;

Hebrews 1:3

BECAUSE OF WHAT HE HAS DONE:

HIS INCARNATION

And without controversy great is the mystery of godliness: God was manifest in the flesh, justified in the Spirit, seen of angels, preached unto the Gentiles, believed on in the world, received up into glory.

1 Timothy 3:16

For unto us a child is born, unto us a son is given: and the government shall be upon his shoulder: and his name shall be called Wonderful, Counsellor, The mighty God, The everlasting Father, The Prince of Peace.

Isaiah 9:6

FOR HIS HOLY LIFE OF PERFECT OBEDIENCE:
Joh. 17:4; Matt.3:17; Joh.8:29

FOR HIS VOLUNTARY AND SUBSTITUTIONARY SACRIFICE ON OUR BEHALF:
Mark 10:45; Joh.10:17-18; Phil.2:5-8; 1Pet 1:11; Rev.1:18; Rom. 6:9-10

BECAUSE OF WHAT HE IS DOING:
He is our Advocate, Intercessor and High Priest
Joh. 2:1; Heb.7:25; 8:1-3;

He is head of the Church.
Eph.1:22-23; 4:8-12,15,16

BECAUSE OF WHAT HE IS GOING TO DO:
His coming.
Joh. 14:1-3; Act.1:10-11; 1Thess. 4:13-18; 1 Cor. 15:51

CHAPTER VII

WHO CAN PRAISE THE LORD?

Only those who are in Christ in this age and only those who trusted God by faith in the Old Testament. It is, however, not as easy as I have indicated above, because we as Christians can only fellowship with God in worship if we are in right standing. This is explained under the following headings:

THOSE WHO HAVE REDEMPTION

We must be redeemed before we can go to Him who is holy. There must be a divinely accepted substitutionary sacrifice.

> For the life of the flesh is in the blood: and I have given it to you upon the altar to make an atonement for your souls: for it is the blood that maketh an atonement for the soul.
>
> **Leviticus 17:11**

> And almost all things are by the law purged with blood; and without shedding of blood is no remission.
>
> **Hebrews 9:22**

That sacrifice must be with blood. There can be no approach to God, no pardon from God and worship to God, apart from an acceptable substitutionary sacrifice which bears the sinner's sins, takes his place, died in his stead and is accepted by God on his behalf. Only Jesus fulfilled these requirements and He did it with His blood. We are now in a position to worship because the perfect Lamb shed His blood and the sacrifice has been accepted.

> Being justified freely by his grace through the redemption that is in Christ Jesus:
>
> **Romans 3:24**

This is the only ground by which the believer can approach God in worship.

THOSE WHO HAVE RELATIONSHIP

Those who approach God do it with "Father" on their lips. It is the Father that seeks worship from His children.

> **But the hour cometh, and now is, when the true worshippers shall worship the Father in spirit and in truth: for the Father seeketh such to worship him.**
>
> **John 4:23**
>
> **Having therefore, brethren, boldness to enter into the holiest by the blood of Jesus,**
>
> **Hebrews 10:19**

It is as "brethren" or those in the family of God that we have boldness to enter the Holiest by the blood of Jesus.

> **For ye have not received the spirit of bondage again to fear; but ye have received the Spirit of adoption, whereby we cry, Abba, Father.**
>
> **Romans 8:15**

The Christian comes, not to a cold impersonal God but to one whom he knows and loves as Father. He knows God as "Abba, Father."

THOSE WHO HAVE REPRESENTATION

The worshipper must have a High Priest as his representative in the presence of God. Through the mediation of the Great High Priest, his worship is made acceptable and presented to God. Our representation is made by Jesus who offered a "better sacrifice,"

> It was therefore necessary that the patterns of things in the heavens should be purified with these; but the heavenly things themselves with better sacrifices than these.
>
> Hebrews 9:23

by which he brought in a "better covenant,"

> But now hath he obtained a more excellent ministry, by how much also he is the mediator of a better covenant, which was established upon better promises.
>
> Hebrews 8:6

which contained "better promises" of better promises of better things,

> And to Jesus the mediator of the new covenant, and to the blood of sprinkling, that speaketh better things than that of Abel.
>
> Hebrews 12:24

resulting in a better hope,

> For the law made nothing perfect, but the bringing in of a better hope did; by the which we draw nigh unto God.
>
> Hebrews 7:19

and leading to a "better country."

> But now they desire a better country, that is, an heavenly: wherefore God is not ashamed to be called their God: for he hath prepared for them a city.
>
> Hebrews 11:16

Our representation has already been made forever, not only by the offer (High Priest) but the offering (who was our High Priest). Christ is thus our Divine Representative in the presence of God. He has secured our redemption by His own precious blood. He has made our relationship actual with God and He now, in His position as our Great High Priest, represents us before the Father's throne. Thus the three-fold ground of worship, which the holiness of the Triune Godhead demanded, has been perfectly and gloriously provided. The redeemed child of God need not stand outside in fear but with holy boldness draws near into the Holiest of all. He is assured that his Representative, the Great High Priest, will present his worship before the Father in all the perfection of His own Person.

For the New Testament age, Jesus gave the answer in John 4:21. Jesus was actually saying that it doesn't matter where you choose to praise. There is no need to be restricted to any building or time. Since we are "of the Spirit" all the time we can worship "in spirit" all the time. Location has nothing to do with it, because we are the worshipping location, we are the temples. We praise the Lord from within.

WHAT ARE THE RESULTS OF PRAISE?

Then Moses said unto Aaron, This is it that the LORD spake, saying, I will be sanctified in them that come nigh me, and before all the people I will be glorified. And Aaron held his peace.

Leviticus 10:3

There can be no greater occupation for man than to glorify God and this is what praise does. The supreme fullness of any individual's purpose is to be totally absorbed in the person of God and to view life through eyes that are filled with the wonder and glory of God's attributes. As we personify all that God is (that is, His glory) we will glorify Him. When blood-redeemed people praise Him, the purposes of the Triune Godhead for man are thus fulfilled and He is glorified. The Father will be glorified in the revelation He has given of Himself in the Son of His love.

The Son will be glorified in the work He has accomplished by the sacrifice of Himself. The Holy Spirit will be glorified for it was through Him that the written revelation came, and His indwelling presence makes possible the worship of the believer. Thus praise rebounds to the glory of the Father, Son and the Holy Spirit.

THE PRAISER WILL BE BLESSED AND JOYFUL

No one loses by giving to God, for God will be no man's debtor. God will pour back to the believer

> Give, and it shall be given unto you; good measure, pressed down, and shaken together, and running over, shall men give into your bosom. For with the same measure that ye mete withal it shall be measured to you again.
>
> Luke 6:38

God's own principle of "it is more blessed to give than to receive" works toward us when we praise. God is described as the blessed God. Consequently all who bless Him in praise are blessed by Him in return. Luke's Gospel concludes in a very beautiful way, after describing the ascension of our Lord,

> And they worshipped him, and returned to Jerusalem with great joy: And were continually in the temple, praising and blessing God. Amen.
>
> Luke 24:52-53

Praise and worship enables the believer to know God better, and to appreciate Him more; and this knowledge causes God to become his exceeding joy.

> Then will I go unto the altar of God, unto God my exceeding joy: yea, upon the harp will I praise thee, O God my God.
>
> Psalm 43:4

He who fulfills God's desire for praise and worship shall have his own desire for joy fulfilled. Thus the adoration that ascends to God from the believer to delight God's heart, will be more than recompensed by the blessing descending from God to the believer, which will rejoice his heart. God's definite promise is "Them that honour me, I will honour (I Sam.2:30).

THE PRAISER WILL ENJOY PROMINENCE

People who praise are praised. As Jacob, obviously under the anointing of God, looked into Judah's future he saw his other sons bowing down to Judah. Praise brings prominence; praise glorifies God and God exalts the praiser.

> **Judah, thou art he whom thy brethren shall praise: thy hand shall be in the neck of thine enemies; thy father's children shall bow down before thee.**
>
> **Judah is a lion's whelp: from the prey, my son, thou art gone up: he stooped down, he couched as a lion, and as an old lion; who shall rouse him up?**
>
> **The sceptre shall not depart from Judah, nor a lawgiver from between his feet, until Shiloh come; and unto him shall the gathering of the people be.**
>
> **Genesis 49:8-10**

When people praise the Lord there is reflected in them a character which causes others to depend on them for leadership. It was so with Judah; it will be so with us. Rulership is the inheritance of people of praise. Whether life will be lived in terror or trust will be determined by whether or not we praise the Lord. In a real sense all the prophecies of Jacob for Judah belong to all who have received kinship with Jesus Christ "the Lion of the tribe of Judah."

THE PRAISER IS BEST PREPARED FOR WORSHIP

> **And the LORD spake unto Moses and unto Aaron, saying,**
>
> **Every man of the children of Israel shall pitch by his own standard, with the ensign of their father's house: far off about the tabernacle of the congregation shall they pitch.**

WHO CAN PRAISE THE LORD?

And on the east side toward the rising of the sun shall they of the standard of the camp of Judah pitch throughout their armies: and Nahshon the son of Amminadab shall be captain of the children of Judah.

Numbers 2:1-3

The camp of praise, Judah, was located closest to the entrance to the Tabernacle court yard. Judah was located on the east side, the first tribe to see the rising of the sun. Praise parks us within sight of the gate of worship and continuously leads us into that experience.

THE PRAISER CONTINUES AS A CONQUEROR

The opening words of the Book of Judges are revealing. The Israelites asked the Lord, "who will be the first to go and fight for us against the Canaanites?" The Lord immediately answered "Judah (praise) is to go; I have given the land into their hands. It was the tribe of praise to whom God had granted the victory! And thus Judges 1 records their advanced attack and victory over Canaanites.

Now after the death of Joshua it came to pass, that the children of Israel asked the LORD, saying, Who shall go up for us against the Canaanites first, to fight against them?

And the LORD said, Judah shall go up: behold, I have delivered the land into his hand.

And the LORD was with Judah; and he drave out the inhabitants of the mountain; but could not drive out the inhabitants of the valley, because they had chariots of iron.

Judges 1:1,2,19

In the midst of the chapter 1 verse 19, we read "The Lord was with the men of Judah (praise). And they took possession of the hill country, but they were unable to drive the people from the plains, because they had iron chariots. Praise continually conquers, but when praise retreats, the enemy becomes bold. Judges 1 reveals that though Judah overcame the Canaanites and oppressed them into forced labor, the tribe did not drive them out completely. As long as they acted in accord with their name, they conquered. The moment of mixture was weakness. The fear of natural strength is not what we fight against.

THE ASSEMBLY WILL BE EDIFIED

Not only does praise glorify God and bring blessing to the worshipper himself; but a company of believers, who give praise its proper place, is blessed and edified thereby; for it is fulfilling its God given function. It will be recalled that God in the Tabernacle, and later in the Temple, responded to the praise of His people by filling the place with His glory.

> **Then a cloud covered the tent of the congregation, and the glory of the LORD filled the tabernacle.**
>
> **Exodus 40:34**
>
> **So that the priests could not stand to minister because of the cloud: for the glory of the LORD had filled the house of the LORD.**
>
> **I Kings 8:11**

Whenever believers gather together today with one heart and voice to praise God spiritually, sincerely, and intelligently, they too shall be made to experience what it means for the place to become fragrant with the glory of the Lord. There is no spot nearer to heaven than when the united worship of an assembly of Christians ascends like fragrant incense before the face of God.

When an assembly of believers puts "first things first" the saints are thereby built up in their most holy faith. This, in turn, fits and enables them to fulfill the other purposes God has in mind for His gathered people. An assembly that allows its service for the Lord to crowd out its praise and worship to the Lord not only comes short of God's purpose for it, but the effectiveness of its purpose is curtailed. Both the desire and the ability for true service flows from spiritual praise and worship. It was after Isaiah had seen the glory of the Lord, and had been impressed with the majesty of His Holy presence, that the call and commission for service came, to which he gladly responded "Here am I, send me." (Isa.6:1-8)

THE UNSAVED WILL BE REACHED

As the praising Christian moves among his fellowmen, he will unconsciously carry with him something of God. The Bible points out that "None of us liveth unto himself."

For none of us liveth to himself, and no man dieth to himself.

Romans 14:7

Each life touches some other life, either for good or for evil. Each Christian by impact of his personality, makes an impression upon others. Only as God, through praise, impresses the believer with Himself, can the believer impress others with God. It is this unconscious influence that counts for so much in one's contact with the world.

CHAPTER VIII

SCRIPTURES THAT REVEAL WHO CAN PRAISE THE LORD

Neh.12:43	All the wives and children
Neh. 5;13	All
Psa. 5:11; 85:6	All God's people who trust Him
Psa. 21:1	The king
Psa. 22:23	Those who fear the Lord
Psa. 22:26; 40:16	Those that seek the Lord
Psa. 22:29	The fat
Psa. 24:2-3	The clean hearted
Psa. 24:6	This generation
Psa. 30:4; 145:10	Saints
Psa. 31:23	Lovers of God
Psa. 90:17	Artists, musicians, craftsmen
Psa. 35:10	All my bones
Psa. 36;7; 102:18	One generation to another
Psa. 145:21	All fresh
Psa. 45:11	The beautiful
Psa. 48:11; 97:8	Daughters of Judah
Psa.66:8; 67:3	People
Psa. 67:4; 86:9	Every nation
Psa. 69:34	Every moving thing
Psa. 84:4	Dwellers in His house
Psa. 150:6	Everything that has breath

HOW DO WE PRAISE?

WITH THE RIGHT ATTITUDE

Psa. 1:2; 37:4;11:2; 40:8	Delight
Psa. 2:11; 96:9; 99:1	Fear and trembling
Psa. 9:1	Whole heart
Psa. 9:2	Gladness
Psa. 19:14	Humility
Psa. 27:13-14	Expectation
Psa. 30:12	Sensitivity
Psa. 43:4	Joy
Psa. 25:2	Without shame
Psa. 27:8	Obedience
Psa. 29:1	Generous praise
Psa. 42:1-2; 143:6	Thirst
Psa. 54:6	Willingness
Psa. 89:17	Reverence

WITH INSTRUMENTS

Psa. 81:2	Timbrel
Psa. 150:3	Trumpet
Psa. 81:2	Psaltery
Psa. 144:9	Instruments

WITH SOUND

Psa. 126:2	Laughter
Psa. 32:11; 35:27	Shouting
Psa. 98:4	Loud noise
Psa. 35:28	Speaking
Psa. 18:3	Calling upon Him
Psa. 33:3	Skillful sound

SCRIPTURES THAT REVEAL WHO CAN PRAISE THE LORD

Psa. 66:1	Noisily
Psa. 92:3	Solemn sound
Psa. 5:11	Shout of joy
Psa. 40:3	New song
Psa. 28:7	Singing

WITH OUR BODIES

Psa. 47:1	Clapping
Psa. 34:1; 71:8	With my mouth
Psa. 63:4	Lifting hands
Psa. 135:2; 24:3	Standing
Psa. 63:3	My lips
Psa. 149:3	Dancing
Psa. 95:6	Bowing and kneeling
Psa. 35:28; 51:14	With my tongue
Psa. 5:3	Waking up
Psa. 46:10	Being still
Psa. 96:7	By giving

CHAPTER IX

MORE SCRIPTURE REFERENCES

For examples of references found on these subjects in the Bible, please study all of the following:

Old Testament

JOSHUA 34:14
For thou shalt worship no other God: for the Lord, whose name is Jealous, is a jealous God.

JOSHUA 5:14
And he said, Nay; but as captain of the host of the Lord am I now come. And Joshua fell on his face to the earth, and did worship, and said unto him, What saith my lord unto his servant?

JUDGES 5:1
Then sang Deborah and Barak the son of Ahinoam on that day.

JUDGES 5:3
Hear, O ye kings; give ear, O ye princes; I, even I, will sing unto the Lord; I will sing praise to the Lord God of Israel.

I SAMUEL 2:1
And Hannah prayed, and said, My heart rejoiceth in the Lord, mine horn is exalted in the Lord: my mouth is enlarged over mine enemies; because I rejoice in thy salvation.

II Samuel 7:26
And let thy name be magnified for ever, saying, The Lord of hosts is the God over Israel: and let the house of thy servant David be established before thee.

THE MECHANICS OF TRUE WORSHIP

II SAMUEL 22:47
The Lord liveth; and blessed be my rock; and exalted be the God of the rock of my salvation.

II KINGS 17:36
But the Lord, who brought you up out of the land of Egypt with great power and a stretched out arm, him shall ye fear, and him shall ye worship, and to him shall ye do sacrifice.

I CHRONICLES 16:8, 9, 10
Give thanks unto the Lord, call upon his name, make known his deeds among the people.

Sing unto him, sing psalms unto him, talk ye of all his wondrous works.

Glory ye in his holy name: let the heart of them rejoice that seek the Lord.

I CHRONICLES 16:24, 25
Declare his glory among the heathen; his marvellous works among all nations.

For great is the Lord, and greatly to be praised: he also is to be feared above all gods.

I CHRONICLES 16:29
Give unto the Lord the glory due unto his name: bring an offering, and come before him: worship the Lord in the beauty of holiness.

I CHRONICLES 16:34
O give thanks unto the Lord; for he is good; for his mercy endureth for ever.

I CHRONICLES 23:5
Moreover four thousand were porters; and four thousand praised the Lord with the instruments which I made, said David, to praise therewith.

MORE SCRIPTURE REFERENCES

I Chronicles 29:11
Thine, O Lord, is the greatness, and the power, and the glory, and the victory, and the majesty: for all that is in the heaven and in the earth is thine; thine is the kingdom, O Lord, and thou art exalted as head above all.

I Chronicles 29:13
Now therefore, our God, we thank thee, and praise thy glorious name.

II Chronicles 5:12
Also the Levites which were the singers, all of them of Asaph, of Heman, of Jeduthun, with their sons and their brethren, being arrayed in white linen, having cymbals and psalteries and harps, stood at the east end of the altar, and with them an hundred and twenty priests sounding with trumpets.

II Chronicles 20:21, 22
And when he had consulted with the people, he appointed singers unto the Lord, and that should praise the beauty of holiness, as they went out before the army, and to say, Praise the Lord; for his mercy endureth for ever.

II Chronicles 23:13
And she looked, and, behold, the king stood at his pillar at the entering in, and the princes and the trumpets by the king: and all the people of the land rejoiced, and sounded with trumpets, also the singers with instruments of musick, and such as taught to sing praise. Then Athaliah rent her clothes, and said, Treason, Treason.

Job 21:12
They take the timbrel and harp, and rejoice at the sound of the organ.

Psalm 5:7
But as for me, I will come into thy house in the multitude of thy mercy: and in thy fear will I worship toward thy holy temple.

Psalm 7:17
I will praise the Lord according to his righteousness: and will sing praise to the name of the Lord most high.

THE MECHANICS OF TRUE WORSHIP

PSALM 9:1, 2
I will praise thee, O Lord, with my whole heart; I will shew forth all thy marvellous works.

I will be glad and rejoice in thee: I will sing praise to thy name, O thou most High.

PSALM 18:46
The Lord liveth; and blessed be my rock; and let the God of my salvation be exalted.

PSALM 18:49
Therefore will I give thanks unto thee, O Lord, among the heathen, and sing praises unto thy name.

PSALM 21:13
Be thou exalted, Lord, in thine own strength: so will we sing and praise thy power.

PSALM 22:22-29
I will declare thy name unto my brethren: in the midst of the congregation will I praise thee.

Ye that fear the Lord, praise him; all ye the seed of Jacob, glorify him; and fear him, all ye the seed of Israel.

For he hath not despised nor abhorred the affliction of the afflicted; neither hath he hid his face from him; but when he cried unto him, he heard.

My praise shall be of thee in the great congregation: I will pay my vows before them that fear him.

The meek shall eat and be satisfied: they shall praise the Lord: and all the kindreds of the nations shall worship before thee.

For the kingdom is the Lord's: and he is the governor among the nations.

MORE SCRIPTURE REFERENCES

All they that be fat upon earth shall eat and worship: all they that go down to the dust shall bow before him: and non can keep alive his own soul.

PSALM 27:6
And now shall mine head be lifted up above mine enemies round about me: therefore will I offer in his tabernacle sacrifices of joy; I will sing, yea, I will sing praises unto the Lord.

PSALM 28:7
The Lord is my strength and my shield; my heart trusted in him, and I am helped: therefore my heart greatly rejoiceth; and with my song will I praise him.

PSALM 29:2
Give unto the Lord the glory due unto his name; worship the Lord in the beauty of holiness.

PSALM 30:11, 12
Thou hast turned for me my mourning into dancing: thou hast put off my sackcloth, and girded me with gladness;

To the end that my glory may sing praise to thee, and not be silent, O Lord my God, I will give thanks unto thee for ever.

PSALM 32:11
Be glad in the Lord, and rejoice ye righteous: and shout for joy, all ye that are upright in heart.

PSALM 33:1-4
Rejoice in the Lord, O ye righteous: for praise is comely for the upright.

Praise the Lord with harp: sing unto him with the psaltery and an instrument of ten strings.

Sing unto him a new song; play skillfully with a loud noise.

For the word of the Lord is right; and all his works are done in truth.

PSALM 34:1, 2, 3
I will bless the Lord at all times: his praise shall continually be in my mouth.

My soul shall make her boast in the Lord: the humble shall hear thereof, and be glad.

O magnify the Lord with me, and let us exalt his name together.

PSALM 35:18
I will give thanks in the great congregation: I will praise thee among much people.

PSALM 35:27, 28
Let them shout for joy, and be glad, that favour my righteous cause: yea, let them say continually, Let the Lord be magnified, which hath pleasure in the prosperity of his servant.

And my tongue shall speak of thy righteousness and of thy praise all the day long.

PSALM 40:3
Let all those that seek thee rejoice and be glad in thee: let such as love thy salvation say continually, The Lord be magnified.

PSALM 43:4, 5
Then will I go unto the altar of God, unto God my exceeding joy: yea, upon the harp will I praise thee, O God my God.

Why art thou cast down, O my soul? and why art thou disquieted within me? hope in God: for I shall yet praise him, who is the health of my countenance, and my God.

PSALM 48:1
Great is the Lord, and greatly to be praised in the city of our God, in the mountain of his holiness.

MORE SCRIPTURE REFERENCES

PSALM 50:23
Whoso offereth praise glorifieth me: and to him that ordereth his conversation aright will I shew the salvation of God.

PSALM 54:6
I will freely sacrifice unto thee: I will praise thy name, O Lord; for it is good.

PSALM 56:10, 11, 12
In God will I praise his word: in the Lord will I praise his word.

In God have I put my trust: I will not be afraid what man can do unto me.

Thy vows are upon me, O God: I will render praises unto thee.

PSALM 57:5
Be thou exalted, O God, above the heavens; let thy glory be above all the earth.

PSALM 57:7
My heart is fixed, O God, my heart is fixed: I will sing and give praise.

PSALM 57:9
I will praise thee, O Lord, among the people: I will sing unto thee among the nations.

PSALM 63:1-7
O God, thou art my God; early will I seek thee: my soul thirsteth for thee, my flesh longeth for thee in a dry and thirsty land, where no water is;

To see thy power and thy glory, so as I have seen thee in the sanctuary.

Because thy lovingkindness is better than life, my lips shall praise thee.

Thus will I bless thee while I live: I will lift up my hands in thy name.

My soul shall be satisfied with marrow and fatness; and my mouth shall praise thee with joyful lips:

When I remember thee upon my bed, and meditate on thee in the night watches.

Because thou hast been my help, therefore in the shadow of thy wings will I rejoice.

PSALM 66:1-8
Make a joyful noise unto God, all ye lands:

Sing forth the honour of his name: make his praise glorious.

Say unto God, How terrible art thou in thy works! through the greatness of thy power shall thine enemies submit themselves unto thee.

All the earth shall worship thee, and shall sing unto thee; they shall sing to thy name. Selah.

Come and see the works of God: he is terrible in his doing toward the children of men.

He turned the sea into dry land: they went through the flood on foot: there did we rejoice in him.

He ruleth by his power for ever; his eyes behold the nations: let not the rebellious exalt themselves. Selah.

O bless our God, ye people, and make the voice of his praise to be heard.

PSALM 67:3
Let the people praise thee, O God; let all the people praise thee.

PSALM 67:5
Let the people praise thee, O God; let all the people praise thee.

PSALM 68:3, 4

MORE SCRIPTURE REFERENCES

But let the righteous be glad; let them rejoice before God: yea, let them exceedingly rejoice.

Sing unto God, sing praises to his name: extol him that rideth upon the heavens by his name JAH, and rejoice before him.

PSALM 69:30-34
I will praise the name of God with a song, and will magnify him with thanksgiving.

This also shall please the Lord better than ox or bullock that hath horns and hoofs.

The humble shall see this, and be glad: and your heart shall live that seek God.

For the Lord heareth the poor, and despiseth not his prisoners.

Let the heaven and earth praise him, the seas, and every thing that moveth therein.

PSALM 70:4
Let all those that seek thee rejoice and be glad in thee: and let such as love thy salvation say continually, Let God be magnified.

PSALM 71:8
Let my mouth be filled with thy praise and with thy honour all the day.

PSALM 71:14
But I will hope continually, and will yet praise thee more and more.

PSALM 71:22
I will also praise thee with the psaltery, even thy truth, O my God: unto thee will I sing with the harp, O thou Holy One of Israel.

THE MECHANICS OF TRUE WORSHIP

PSALM 81:1
Sing aloud unto God our strength: make a joyful noise unto the God of Jacob.

PSALM 86:12
I will praise thee, O Lord my God, with all my heart: and I will glorify thy name for evermore.

PSALM 89:5
And the heavens shall praise thy wonders, O Lord: thy faithfulness also in the congregation of the saints.

PSALM 89:16
In thy name shall they rejoice all the day: and in thy righteousness shall they be exalted.

PSALM 92:1-3
It is a good thing to give thanks unto the Lord, and to sing praises unto thy name, O most High:

To shew forth my lovingkindness in the morning, and thy faithfulness every night,

Upon an instrument of ten strings, and upon the psaltery; upon the harp with a solemn sound.

PSALM 95:1-7
O come, let us sing unto the Lord: let us make a joyful noise to the rock of our salvation.

Let us come before his presence with thanksgiving, and make a joyful noise unto him with psalms.

For the Lord is a great God, and a great King above all gods.

In his hand are the deep places of the earth: the strength of the hills is his also.

MORE SCRIPTURE REFERENCES

The sea is his, and he made it: and his hands formed the dry land.

O come, let us worship and bow down: let us kneel before the Lord our maker.

For he is our God; and we are the people of his pasture, and the sheep of his hand ...

PSALM 96:1-13

O sing unto the Lord a new song: sing unto the Lord, all the earth.

Sing unto the Lord, bless his name; shew forth his salvation from day to day.

Declare his glory among the heathen, his wonders among all people.

For the Lord is great, and greatly to be praised: he is to be feared above all gods.

For all the gods of the nations are idols: but the Lord made the heavens.

Honour and majesty are before him: strength and beauty are in his sanctuary.

Give unto the Lord, O ye kindreds of the people, give unto the Lord glory and strength.

Give unto the Lord the glory due unto his name: bring an offering, and come into his courts.

O worship the Lord in the beauty of holiness: fear before him, all the earth.

Say among the heathen that the Lord reigneth: the world also shall be established that it shall not be moved: he shall judge the people righteously.

Let the heavens rejoice, and let the earth be glad; let the sea roar, and the fulness thereof.

THE MECHANICS OF TRUE WORSHIP

Let the field be joyful, and all that is therein: then shall all the trees of the wood rejoice

Before the Lord: for he cometh, for he cometh to judge the earth: he shall judge the world with righteousness, and the people with his truth.

PSALM 97:9
For thou, Lord, art high above all the earth: thou art exalted far above all gods.

PSALM 98:1-6
O sing unto the Lord a new song; for he hath done marvellous things: his right hand, and his holy arm, hath gotten him the victory.

The Lord hath made known his salvation: his righteousness hath he openly shewed in the sight of the heathen.

He hath remembered his mercy and his truth toward the house of Israel: all the ends of the earth have seen the salvation of our God.

Make a joyful noise unto the Lord, all the earth: make a loud noise, and rejoice, and sing praise.

Sing unto the Lord with the harp; with the harp, and the voice of a psalm.

With trumpets and sound of cornet make a joyful noise before the Lord, the King.

PSALM 99:3
Let them praise thy great and terrible name; for it is holy.

PSALM 99:5
Exalt ye the Lord our God, and worship at his footstool; for he is holy.

MORE SCRIPTURE REFERENCES

PSALM 99:9
Exalt the Lord our God, and worship at his holy hill, for the Lord our God is holy.

PSALM 100:1-5
Make a joyful noise unto the Lord, all ye lands.

Serve the Lord with gladness: come before his presence with singing.

Know ye that the Lord he is God: it is he that hath made us, and not we ourselves; we are his people, and the sheep of his pasture.

Enter into his gates with thanksgiving, and into his courts with praise: be thankful unto him, and bless his name.

For the Lord is good; his mercy is everlasting; and his truth endureth to all generations.

PSALM 104:33
I will sing unto the Lord as long as I live: will sing praise to my God while I have my being.

PSALM 105:2
Sing unto him, sing psalms unto him: talk ye of all his wondrous works.

PSALM 106:1
Praise ye the Lord. O give thanks unto the Lord; for he is good: for his mercy endureth for ever.

PSALM 106:12
Then believed they his words; they sang his praise.

PSALM 107:8
Oh that men would praise the Lord for his goodness, and for his wondrous works to the children of men!

PSALM 107:32

Let them exalt him also in the congregation of the people, and praise him in the assembly of the elders.

PSALM 108:1
O God, my heart is fixed; I will sing and give praise, even with my glory.

PSALM 108:3
I will praise thee, O Lord, among the people: and I will sing praises unto thee among the nations.

PSALM 109:30
I will greatly praise the Lord with my mouth; yea I will praise him among the multitude.

PSALM 111:1
Praise ye the Lord. I will praise the Lord with my whole heart, in the assembly of the upright, and in the congregation.

PSALM 112:1
Praise ye the Lord. Blessed is the man that feareth the Lord, that delighteth greatly in his commandments.

PSALM 113:1
Praise ye the Lord. Praise, O ye servants of the Lord, praise the name of the Lord.

PSALM 117:1, 2
O praise the Lord, all ye nations: praise him, all ye people.

For his merciful kindness is great toward us: and the truth of the Lord endureth for ever. Praise ye the Lord.

PSALM 118:19
Open to me the gates of righteousness: I will go into them, and I will praise the Lord.

MORE SCRIPTURE REFERENCES

PSALM 118:21
I will praise thee: for thou hast heard me, and art become my salvation.

PSALM 118:28
Thou art my God, and I will praise thee: thou art my God, I will exalt thee.

PSALM 119:7
I will praise thee with uprightness of heart, when I shall have learned thy righteous judgments.

PSALM 119:175
Let my soul live, and it shall praise thee; and let thy judgments help me.

PSALM 135:1
Praise ye the Lord. Praise ye the name of the Lord; praise him, O ye servants of the Lord.

PSALM 135:3
Praise the Lord; for the Lord is good: sing praises unto his name; for it is pleasant.

PSALM 135:21
Blessed be the Lord out of Zion, which dwelleth at Jerusalem. Praise ye the Lord.

PSALM 138:1, 2
I will praise thee with my whole heart: before the gods will I sing praise unto thee.

I will worship toward thy holy temple, and praise thy name for thy lovingkindness and for thy truth: for thou hast magnified thy word above all thy name.

PSALM 138:4
All the kings of the earth shall praise thee, O Lord, when they hear the words of thy mouth.

THE MECHANICS OF TRUE WORSHIP

PSALM 139:14
I will praise thee; for I am fearfully and wonderfully made: marvellous are thy works; and that my soul knoweth right well.

PSALM 144:9
I will sing a new song unto thee, O God: upon a psaltery and an instrument of ten strings will I sing praises unto thee.

PSALM 145:1-4
I will extol thee, my God, O king; and I will bless thy name for ever and ever.

Every day will I bless thee; and I will praise thy name for ever and ever.

Great is the Lord, and greatly to be praised; and his greatness is unsearchable.

One generation shall praise thy works to another, and shall declare thy mighty acts.

PSALM 145:10
All thy works shall praise thee, O Lord; and thy saints shall bless thee.

PSALM 145:21
My mouth shall speak the praise of the Lord: and let all flesh bless his holy name for ever and ever.

PSALM 146:1, 2
Praise ye the Lord. Praise the Lord, O my soul.

While I live will I praise the Lord: I will sing praises unto my God while I have any being.

PSALM 146:10
The Lord shall reign for ever, even thy God, O Zion, unto all generations. Praise ye the Lord.

PSALM 147:1

MORE SCRIPTURE REFERENCES

Praise ye the Lord: for it is good to sing praises unto our God; for it is pleasant; and praise is comely.

PSALM 147:12
Praise the Lord, O Jerusalem; praise thy God, O Zion.

PSALM 147:20
He hath not dealt so with any nation: and as for his judgments, they have not known them. Praise ye the Lord.

PSALM 148:1-4
Praise ye the Lord. Praise ye the Lord from the heavens: praise him in the heights.

Praise ye him, all his angels: praise ye him, all his hosts.

Praise ye him, sun and moon: praise him, all ye stars of light.

Praise him, ye heavens of heavens, and ye waters that be above the heavens.

Let them praise the name of the Lord: for he commanded, and they were created.

PSALM 148:13, 14
Let them praise the name of the Lord: for his name alone is excellent; his glory is above the earth and heaven.

He also exalteth the horn of his people, the praise of all his saints; even of the children of Israel, a people near unto him. Praise ye the Lord.

PSALM 149:1
Praise ye the Lord. Sing unto the Lord a new song, and his praise in the congregation of saints.

PSALM 149:3
Let them praise his name in the dance: let them sing praises unto him with the timbrel and harp.

PSALM 149:6
Let the high praises of God be in their mouth, and a two-edged sword in their hand.

PSALM 150:1-6
Praise ye the Lord. Praise God in his sanctuary: praise him in the firmament of his power.

Praise him for his mighty acts: praise him according to his excellent greatness.

Praise him with the sound of the trumpet: praise him with the psaltery and harp.

Praise him with the timbrel and dance: praise him with stringed instruments and organs.

Praise him upon the loud cymbals: praise him upon the high sounding cymbals.

Let every thing that hath breath praise the Lord. Praise ye the Lord.

PROVERB 27:2
Let another man praise thee, and not thine own mouth; a stranger, and not thine own lips.

PROVERB 27:21
As the fining pot for silver, and the furnace for gold; so is a man to his praise.

PROVERB 28:4
They that forsake the law praise the wicked: but such as keep the law contend with them.

ISAIAH 2:2

MORE SCRIPTURE REFERENCES

And it shall come to pass in the last days, that the mountain of the Lord's house shall be established in the top of the mountains, and shall be exalted above the hills; and all nations shall flow unto it.

Isaiah 12:4
And in that day shall ye say, Praise the Lord, call upon his name, declare his doings among the people, make mention that his name is exalted.

Isaiah 13:2
Lift ye up a banner upon the high mountain, exalt the voice unto them, shake the hand, that they may go into the gates of the nobles.

Isaiah 25:1
O Lord, thou art my God; I will exalt thee, I will praise thy name; for thou hast done wonderful things; thy counsels of old are faithfulness and truth.

Isaiah 33:5
The Lord is exalted; for he dwelleth on high: he hath filled Zion with judgment and righteousness.

Isaiah 38:18, 19
For the grave cannot praise thee, death can not celebrate thee: they that go down into the pit cannot hope for they truth.

The living, the living, he shall praise thee, as I do this day: the father to the children shall make known thy truth.

Isaiah 42:10
Sing unto the Lord a new song, and his praise from the end of the earth, ye that go down to the sea, and all that is therein; the isles, and the inhabitants thereof.

Isaiah 42:12
Let them give glory unto the Lord, and declare his praise in the islands.

Isaiah 43:21
This people have I formed for myself; they shall shew forth my praise.

Isaiah 61:3
To appoint unto them that mourn in Zion, to give unto them beauty for ashes, the oil of joy for mourning, the garment of praise for the spirit of heaviness; that they might be called trees of righteousness, the planting of the Lord, that he might be glorified.

Isaiah 61:11
For as the earth bringeth forth her bud, and as the garden causeth the things that are sown in it to spring forth; so the Lord God will cause righteousness and praise to spring forth before all the nations.

Jeremiah 20:13
Sing unto the Lord, praise ye the Lord: for he hath delivered the soul of the poor from the hand of evildoers.

Jeremiah 26:2
Thus saith the Lord; Stand in the court of the Lord's house, and speak unto all the cities of Judah, which come to worship in the Lord's house, all the words that I command thee to speak unto them; diminish not a word.

Jeremiah 31:7
For thus saith the Lord; Sing with gladness for Jacob, and shout among the chief of the nations: publish ye, praise ye, and say, O Lord, save thy people, the remnant of Israel.

Jeremiah 33:9
And it shall be to me a name of joy, a praise and an honour before all the nations of the earth, which shall hear all the good that I do unto them: and they shall fear and tremble for all the goodness and for all the prosperity that I procure unto it.

Jeremiah 33:11
The voice of joy, and the voice of gladness, the voice of the bridegroom, and the voice of the bride, the voice of them that shall say, Praise the Lord of hosts: for the Lord is good; for his mercy endureth for ever: and of them that

shall bring the sacrifice of praise into the house of the Lord. For I will cause to return the captivity of the land, as at the first, saith the Lord.

New Testament

MATTHEW 15:9
But in vain they do worship me, teaching for doctrines the commandments of men.

MATTHEW 21:16
And said unto him, Hearest thou what these say? And Jesus saith unto them, Yea; have ye never read, Out of the mouth of babes and sucklings thou hast perfected praise?

LUKE 4:8
And Jesus answered and said unto him, Get thee behind me, Satan: for it is written, Thou shalt worship the Lord thy God, and him only shalt thou serve.

LUKE 18:43
And immediately he received his sight, and followed him, glorifying God: and all the people, when they saw it, gave praise unto God.

LUKE 19:37
And when he was come nigh, even now at the descent of the mount of Olives, the whole multitude of the disciples began to rejoice and praise God with a loud voice for all the mighty works that they had seen.

JOHN 4:24
God is a spirit: and they that worship him must worship him in spirit and in truth.

ROMANS 15:11
And again, Praise the Lord, all ye Gentiles; and laud him, all ye people.

I CORINTHIANS 4:5

Therefore judge nothing before the time, until the Lord come, who both will bring to light the hidden things of darkness, and will make manifest the counsels of the hearts: and then shall every man have praise of God.

EPHESIANS 1:6
To the praise of the glory of his grace, wherein he hath made us accepted in the beloved.

EPHESIANS 1:12
That we should be to the praise of his glory, who first trusted in Christ.

EPHESIANS 1:14
Which is the earnest of our inheritance until the redemption of the purchased possession, unto the praise of his glory.

EPHESIANS 5:19
Speaking to yourselves in psalms and hymns and spiritual songs, singing and making melody in your heart to the Lord.

PHILIPPIANS 1:11
Being filled with the fruits of righteousness, which are by Jesus Christ, unto the glory and praise of God.

PHILIPPIANS 3:3
For we are the circumcision, which worship God in the spirit, and rejoice in Christ Jesus, and have no confidence in the flesh.

PHILIPPIANS 4:8
Finally, brethren, whatsoever things are true, whatsoever things are honest, whatsoever things are just, whatsoever things are pure, whatsoever things are lovely, whatsoever things are of good report; if there be any virtue, and if there be any praise, think on these things.

COLOSSIANS 2:23
Which things have indeed a shew of wisdom in will worship, and humility, and neglecting of the body; not in any honour to the satisfying of the flesh.

MORE SCRIPTURE REFERENCES

HEBREWS 1:6
And again, when he bringeth in the firstbegotten into the world, he saith, And let all the angels of God worship him.

HEBREWS 2:12
Saying, I will declare thy name unto my brethren, in the midst of the church I will sing praise unto thee.

HEBREWS 13:15
By him therefore let us offer the sacrifice of praise to God continually, that is, the fruit of our lips giving thanks to his name.

I PETER 1:7
That the trial of your faith, being much more precious than of gold that perisheth, though it be tried with fire, might be found unto praise and honour and glory at the appearing of Jesus Christ.

I PETER 4:11
If any man speak, let him speak as the oracles of God; if any man minister, let him do it as of the ability which God giveth; that God in all things may be glorified through Jesus Christ, to whom be praise and dominion for ever and ever. Amen.

I PETER 5:6
Humble yourselves therefore under the mighty hand of God, that he may exalt you in due time.

REVELATION 5:11-14
And I beheld, and I heard the voice of many angels round about the throne and the beasts and the elders: and the number of them was ten thousand times ten thousand, and thousands of thousands;

Saying with a loud voice, Worthy is the Lamb that was slain to receive power, and riches, and wisdom, and strength, and honour, and glory, and blessing.

And every creature which is in heaven, and on the earth, and under the earth, and such as are in the sea, and all that are in them, heard I saying, Blessing, and honour, and glory, and power, be unto him that sitteth upon the throne, and unto the Lamb for ever and ever.

And the four beasts said, Amen. And the four and twenty elders fell down and worshippped him that liveth for ever and ever.

REVELATION 7:11, 12
And all the angels stood round about the throne, and about the elders and the four beasts, and fell before the throne on their faces, and worshipped God,

Saying, Amen: Blessing, and glory, and wisdom, and thanksgiving, and honour, and power, and might, be unto our God for ever and ever. Amen.

REVELATION 14:7
Saying with a loud voice, Fear God, and give glory to him; for the hour of his judgment is come: and worship him that made heaven, and earth, and the sea, and the fountains of waters.

REVELATION 15:4
Who shall not fear thee, O Lord, and glorify thy name? for thou only art holy: for all nations shall come and worship before thee; for thy judgments are made manifest.

REVELATION 19:5
And a voice came out of the throne, saying, Praise our God, all ye his servants, and ye that fear him, both small and great.

CHAPTER X

A PRAYER FOR YOU

Father God, in the Name of Jesus, I pray that You would release a renewed strength to worship You. As you continue to demonstrate and reveal who you are in My life, I will be one that You may count on to worship You. I ask that You allow Your divine enablement--You grace, to fully engulf me, that I might worship You in Spirit and in Truth!

I pray that You continue to life me with the truths of this book in the How To's of praising and worshipping You. I decree and declare that I will put into practice, what I have learned.

I come against every hinderance that would prevent me from worshipping You, in Jesus' name.

Father, from this day forth, I declare that I will consistently enter into Your presence and praise and worship You holy name.

I confess that I am a true worshipper and possess a heart cry and hunger for the things of God, in Jesus' name, Amen!